CRASH COURSE Electric Guitar

Jamie Humphries

smt

Electric Guitar

Printed and bound in the UK

Published in the UK by SMT, an imprint of Bobcat Books Limited
14-15 Berners Street, London W1T 3LJ

www.musicsales.com

Cover image: Alamy

ISBN: 1-84492-068-2

SMT1452R

CONTENTS

ABOUT THE AUTHOR

Jamie Humphries started playing guitar at the tender age of five. Throughout his school and college years, he cut his teeth in various covers and original bands. At the beginning of the '90s, he began studying with renowned teacher/music columnist Phil Hilborne.

Before too long, Jamie was teaching privately, as well as gigging regularly. He was then offered a column on the UK magazine *Guitar Techniques*, and later began transcribing for Total Accuracy, writing several books for their highly popular *Jam With...* series. He has also contributed to both *Guitarist* and *Total Guitar* magazines.

Jamie caught the attention of US guitar manufacturer Ernie Ball/Musicman and began working as their UK clinician/demonstrator. He also endorses and demonstrates for revered UK amplifier manufacturer Cornford Amplification. In addition to this, Jamie earned a teaching position at the ACM in Guildford, where he continues to teach.

More recently Jamie has filmed several instructional DVDs for Total Accuracy and Music Sales. He has also written two bestselling titles for SMT, *Giants Of Rock* and *Giants Of Metal*, both of which received excellent reviews and are enjoying massive worldwide sales. He is currently working on his own guitar-tuition show on the new Satellite TV Music Channel and The M Channel. He continues his monthly column for *Guitar Techniques*, contributes lessons and backing tracks for Total Accuracy's Lick Library, and performs on the twice-monthly transcription in drum magazine *Rhythm*.

Electric Guitar

During the course of his career, Jamie has worked with such artists as Richie Kotzen, Vinnie Moore, Ty Tabor, Zakk Wylde, Steve Morse, Albert Lee and Paul Gilbert, and has appeared on television alongside Ronan Keating! He is currently working on a solo album which includes a guest appearance by Richie Kotzen.

www.jamiehumphries.com

ACKNOWLEDGEMENTS

Thanks to...

Sterling Ball, Derek Brooks, Beth Wreden and everyone at Ernie Ball/Musicman guitars.

Paul Cornford, Martin Kidd and everyone at Cornford Amplification.

Rod Bradley, Marc Snelling, Pete Lunney and all the guys at Strings & Things.

Steinberg music-production software.

Russell McVeigh at Netstepper.

John Chandler at Pedal Train.

Cliff Douse and all my friends at *Guitar Techniques* magazine.

Mike Leonard at *Guitarist* magazine.

Kim Waller and Stuart Bull at Total Accuracy/Lick Library.

Everyone at the M Channel.

Phil Brooks, Martin Kennedy and Ian Edwards at the ACM, Guildford.

Jason Campbell (Clunk).

Phil Hilborne

Pete Riley.

Dave Kilminster.

Vinnie Moore.

Richie Kotzen.

Greg Timmons.

Special thanks to my mum and dad, and the rest of my family – Adrian, Emma, Martin, Kylie, and Georgia – for their love and support.

Electric Guitar

All songs and lesson examples by Jamie Humphries, © Jamie Humphries 2004.

Musicians

Guitar, bass, keyboards and programming: Jamie Humphries

Drums on the jam tracks: Pete Riley

Recorded, mixed and mastered by Jamie Humphries at The Corner, Maidstone, Kent.

Drums recorded by Pete Riley at his studio in Witham, Essex.

Jamie Humphries uses and endorses Musicman guitars/Ernie Ball strings, Cornford amplifiers, Dunlop picks and pedals, Pedal Train pedal boards and Steinberg music-production software.

Pete Riley uses and endorses Premier drums, Zildjian cymbals and Vic Firth sticks.

Websites

www.jamiehumphries.com

www.peteriley.net

INTRODUCTION

Welcome to *Crash Course Electric Guitar*. In the past, I've written more band-based projects with my titles *Giants Of Metal* and *Giants Of Rock*. Although both of these books included technical sections, their focus was more on styles of artists rather than on structured practice and study.

OK, I'm sure that the title of this book isn't going to fool you! *Crash Course*? Learn guitar in just eight weeks? You're right – learning any instrument takes years of dedication, hard work and, in some instances, a certain amount of sacrifice. There's no way that, after reading this book, you're going to be a master at electric guitar. But this book does present a good starting block, with study guides ranging from simple chord exercises to full-blown solos. It also offers an organised practice routine that, if followed, will help you maximise practice time and guarantee results. It also includes ideas for the future, with exercises and studies that can be used for the rest of your guitar-playing career.

I considered many factors when constructing the daily practice tasks for this book, including technical ability, musical styles and rewards, but the main factor I considered when writing each module was *time* – something that many of us don't have a lot of. Day-to-day routines of life and work often take precedence over things like guitar practice routines. All I ask, though, is that you try to set aside half an hour or 40 minutes to practise the examples shown here. Think of that wasted time you spend watching junk television you're not really interested in! A lot of the time, putting together a practice routine is just down to good time management.

Electric Guitar

Over the years, I've encountered students of all abilities, some who have been playing for over 20 years but probably haven't improved much since the day they started. This is probably down to an inability to organise their time, and to a reluctance to play new and challenging things. If you spend your time playing the same tired old licks and don't try to push yourself into new areas, you'll never improve. Every time you pick up the guitar, try to play something new. This is the idea behind each of the daily tasks set out in this book.

Anyway, that's enough of my waffling! It's time to get down to some practising and to embark on the first steps of your guitar journey. Good luck!

Jamie Humphries

July 2004

HOW THIS BOOK WORKS

This book presents a series of guitar lesson modules designed to be studied over a period of eight-weeks. There's a lesson per day, giving you a grand total of 56 lessons to work through. The weekly modules gradually become technically more demanding, but don't worry – the gradient isn't too steep. At the end of each week, there's a short test consisting of a few simple questions based on that week's lesson, just to make sure you've been doing your homework...and to make those of you who haven't been paying attention feel a little guilty!

I've also given you a small reward at the end of each week in the form of a full-blown study piece in a particular style. The piece will focus on certain things that you'll have learnt that week and put them into a musical context. The CD contains both full and backing tracks of these study pieces, played by a live band.

By the time you've reached the end of *Crash Course Electric Guitar*, you should have absorbed enough information and have enough technical ability to conquer your favourite songs, start jamming with friends or simply continue learning how to play this incredibly addictive and wonderful instrument. Don't worry – after eight weeks this book won't be ready to spend the rest of its life collecting dust in the loft; many of the examples will continue to be part of your daily practice routine.

 Keep your eyes peeled for logos and signs as you plough ahead. Whenever you see this symbol, for instance, it means that the example is demonstrated on the accompanying CD, which will speed things up a little for you. If your music/tab reading is a little slow to start with, hearing the example played through will help

Electric Guitar

you to grasp the exercise in question and (hopefully) stop you losing interest. The tracks found on the CD include technical exercises, chords and daily studies, as well as your weekly reward for all of your hard work: the full track.

 Whenever you see this symbol, it means that the exercise should be worked at over a long period of time – for example, in exercises concerned with building up picking-hand stamina or synchronising left and right hands. These types of exercises can be used for many years, with the tempo gradually being raised so that stamina builds up over a period of time.

 This symbol is used when a particular exercise should be completed in a set period of time – for example, playing a hammer-on/pull-off exercise for a couple of minutes. Make sure you have a clock or stopwatch where you practise!

 This symbol is used to stress a point, and to make sure it doesn't go in one ear and out the other. These examples are very important, so pay attention!

 This symbol is used at each end-of-week test. Lessons run from Monday to Saturday, and the test takes place on Sunday. Don't worry, it's only a few questions!

 To help you on your way, I've included several quotes from some of the world's greatest guitarists. These little pearls of wisdom are there to inspire you and give you a lift during those dark, lonely hours of practice.

GETTING STARTED

Before we embark on our daily lesson schedule, I thought it would be a good idea to look at the guitar itself and the equipment associated with it. Something I've discovered over my years of teaching is that, although students can have a great knowledge of playing and technique, they often have limited knowledge when it comes to the guitar itself. Knowing the difference between the different types of guitars, styles, pickups, etc, as well as amplifiers and effects, is very important when you're trying to achieve the sound you want.

THE ELECTRIC GUITAR

Choosing the right guitar is very important and is a decision that shouldn't be rushed. There are many factors to consider, but first you have to ask yourself, 'What do I want to achieve from the instrument?' Do you want to join a working band that plays many different styles of music? If so, you'll need a guitar capable of producing many different types of sound.

Do you have a particular style in mind that you're interested in – ie rock, metal, country, jazz or alternative/indie? All of these different styles have their own individual sounds, and often each style will have a certain guitar associated with it – for example, many rock/blues guitarists favour either the Gibson Les Paul or the Fender Stratocaster, while country guitarists often opt for the Telecaster. The metal guitarist will often use some form of Super Strat, like an Ibanez, and will sometimes even choose seven-string models. A jazz guitarist, meanwhile, would possibly choose a semi-acoustic guitar such as a Gibson ES175. Of course, these are only examples, and there are many alternatives to the guitars listed here.

Electric Guitar

First, let's take a look at the guitar's anatomy. I've included some pictures to help you to distinguish between different types of pickup, bridge, fingerboard and other variables.

The guitar is made up of two main parts: the body and the neck. The body houses the *pickups*, *controls* (including the pickup selector switch, volume and tone) and the *bridge*, and can be made from various woods, such as alder, ash or mahogany. The neck, meanwhile, is made up of the *fingerboard* and *frets* (which you hold to produce single notes and chords), the *nut* (through which the strings pass on their way to the *headstock*) and the headstock itself, which includes the *machine heads* (used for tuning the pitch of each of string). The fingerboard can also be made from various types of wood, including maple, rosewood and ebony. The neck can be either bolted onto the body or glued in place (ie a *set neck*) and can also be made from a variety of different woods.

The picture on the left shows my main guitar, which is equipped with a vintage, non-locking tremolo system, or *whammy bar*. It's a particularly versatile guitar; its many different switching possibilities can cover everything from rock to jazz.

Pickups

First, what is a pickup? Well, a pickup is basically a wire-wound magnet that picks up the vibrations of the strings. There are several different types, such as humbuckers, single coils and P90s ('Soapbars'), to name but a few. These are *passive* (ie unpowered) pickups, and there are *active* pickups, which run on 9V batteries and produce a louder, clean sound, although many guitarist argue that they lack character.

The single-coil pickup comprises a single wound magnet and has a very clean, glassy quality, making it great for blues and clean chords. Single-coil pickups can sometimes sound a little transparent and thin, and they also suffer from hum, but they have a great character and tone, and are favoured by many of the world's top guitarists.

The single-coil-pickup guitar

Electric Guitar

The humbucker is made up from two coils and has a very thick, raunchy tone which is great for rock and metal. Because it uses two coils, it cancels hum – hence its name. Many modern rock guitars are wired in such a way that the humbucker coils can be split into single coils, enabling you to get the best of both worlds.

The humbucking pickup

The final type of pickup is the P90, which is essentially a big single-coil pickup that produces a very thick, retro tone. It's a great alternative to a standard single-coil pickup if you want a little more kick and grunt.

Electric Guitar

The P90 'Soapbar' pickup

All of these pickups are controlled by the guitar's pickup-selector switch, which will be either a three- or five-way switch allowing for many pickup-switching permutations. Some guitars feature combinations of single-coil and humbucker pickups, which make for a very versatile instrument.

Bridge

There are two types of bridge: the *fixed bridge* and the *floating bridge*. The fixed bridge is fixed to the body of the guitar, with the strings either passing through the body or secured to the bridge itself, or indeed a separate tailpiece. Fixed bridges

Electric Guitar

are very stable for tuning and produce a very full, rich tone, due to the direct contact with the body of the guitar.

The Fixed bridge

With the other type of bridge – the floating bridge or tremolo system – there are two main types of setup: the *vintage system* and the *double-locking system*. On vintage systems, the tremolo bridge is fixed to the guitar body but is able to pivot and move. In the back of the guitar, the tremolo block is fixed to the body of the guitar via a series of springs which allow the bridge to be raised and lowered and to return to its original pitch. The bridge is moved up and down in pitch with a bar

(also known as an *arm*). This type of bridge is used to raise or lower the pitches of the notes and to produce vibrato effects.

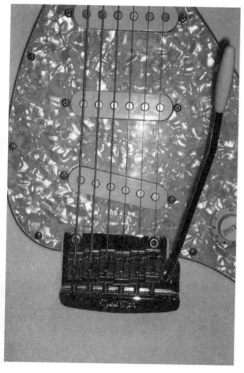

The vintage tremolo system

The tremolo block and springs

Meanwhile, the double-locking system provides a facility for very extreme abuse, allowing the strings to be lowered so much that they literally flop about and yet return to pitch and remain in tune. The strings are locked to the bridge itself, with their ball ends removed, while the nut is replaced with a locking nut, which locks the strings into place, making it pretty impossible for them to go out of tune, although if they do slip, they can be fine-tuned at the bridge. This system was pioneered in the late '70s by the Floyd Rose company and was popularised by rock guitarist Eddie Van Halen.

Electric Guitar

The Floyd Rose system

The locking nut

THE AMPLIFIER

Now that we've looked at the general make-up of the guitar, it's important for you to know what to plug it into if you want to achieve that dream tone. There are two types of amplifier, the *combo* and the *stack*, both of which can be either a valve or transistor model, or a hybrid (ie a mixture of the two). The past few years have also seen a rise in popularity of *amp modellers*, compact units that use digital technology to reproduce the sounds of many different amplifiers.

A combo is basically a combination amplifier (hence the name), with the amplifier and the speaker cabinet housed in one unit. This is a very good starting point, and

this type of amp can be bought relatively cheaply. A valve combo is more expensive than a transistor amp but will produce a much warmer and fuller tone.

A combo amplifier

A *stack* consists of two separate units: the amp head and the speaker enclosure. Stack units are quite expensive, but they do produce a very full tone. This type of system is not for the bedroom guitarist, however, and is suited more to a band situation. Definitely something for the future!

An amp head and cab stack

Electric Guitar

EFFECTS UNITS

Although at this stage effects aren't exactly a high priority, at some point you'll probably feel the need to buy some – all aspiring guitarists do. There are hundreds of types of effects to choose from, but the main units to consider are a delay (ie echo); a modulation pedal; either a chorus, flanger or phaser; and a crunch pedal (ie distortion or overdrive). Pedals can be used to enhance your sound, and can also inspire you when you're writing ideas. U2 guitarist The Edge relies heavily on effects units to produce his legendary sound and style. Here's an example of a typical pedal board, just to whet your appetite!

A typical effects pedal board

STRINGS

here are many different brands of strings, and many different gauges. The only one ue way to find the right strings for you is trial and error. While thinner-gauge trings are easier on the fingers and easier to manipulate and bend, heavier strings ffer a fuller sound, greater tuning stability and, in some cases, less chance of reaking. I would suggest a medium-gauge set of strings – 09mm–42mm is a pretty tandard gauge, for instance, and a very good place for you to start.

PICK OR FINGERS?

Another tricky subject – do you use your fingers or a pick? And, if you choose a pick, how thick or thin should it be? Guitarists such as Jeff Beck and Mark Knopfler use their fingers, and both these players have a very distinctive sound. Indeed, using your fingers can produce some very interesting results, but the pick will enable you to use techniques that using fingers doesn't, such as alternate and sweep picking, and to produce faster and more precise scale-based lines. Some guitarists use a combination of pick and fingers, which enables the benefits of both approaches. Once again, it's down to you to see what works best for you, although I wouldn't advise ditching the pick too early – give it a go for a while. Some players only opt for fingers as they find pick technique too difficult in the beginning, so persevere!

ow onto pick gauges. Thicker picks have a more precise and accurate response but re also a little harder to use when you first start to play, but if your pick is too thin, ou'll lose a lot of attack and power. I would suggest trying somewhere around the nedium-to-heavy mark and try using .8mm- or even 1mm-gauge strings.

Electric Guitar

SUMMARY

Hopefully this section has helped you to understand many of the different types of

guitars, amps and effects that are available, as well as providing a little inside info

on strings and picks.

When you choose a guitar, don't be governed by look and colour; make sure the

instrument has a lively tone when unamplified and that it feels comfortable and

balanced. And don't be fooled by the price; you don't have to spend an arm and a

leg to get a good electric guitar. Many of the top brands offer great value budget

guitars for as little as £150 ($275).

The amp doesn't have to be too extravagant, either. A simple, small combo will

suffice to start with. Once again, many leading companies produce affordable and

practical practice amps, so make sure you get some good advise from your music

shop and don't buy the first thing they offer.

If possible, try to talk to someone who has some guitar-playing experience; most

guitar shops will be able to point you in the right direction. There are also many

guitar magazines on the market that review equipment, so check these out too.

READING MUSIC

I know the question on everyone's lips is: 'Do I have to read music?' Well, it depends on how serious you are. As a professional musician, I read music on a daily basis when I'm either teaching, transcribing or on a gig or session. If you're considering a career in music, then yes, you do need to learn; reading music can open up many doors in the working environment, while it can also help you to play music you wouldn't normally have played, or that you've never heard before.

All of the examples in this book are written in both *standard notation* and *tablature* (a standard form of guitar notation). Tablature – or *tab*, for short – will be explained in a later lesson, but for now it's enough to say that a student can understand tab in a relatively short space of time, while reading standard notation is a lot more involved and takes many months. As the focus here is geared towards playing, I've chosen not to discuss standard notation here, although I would advise you to seek out any of the many books available on the subject.

Another form of guitar notation that's very easy to read is the *chord box*. The six vertical lines here represent the six strings of the guitar, starting with the thickest (ie lowest) and running from left to right to the highest (ie thinnest), and the horizontal lines represent the frets. Chords and scales are notated by dots marked on specific strings and frets where the fingers should be placed. If a string is not to be played, it's marked at the top of the diagram with a cross ('X'), while a circle ('O') denotes an open string.

Electric Guitar

Before we get into our first lesson, it's very important for you know how to practise properly. First of all, your environment – it's no good trying to practise in your front room while the whole family is watching the TV. Try to find a quite spot where you can practise without distraction. Make sure you have a comfortable chair, preferably a stool or some seat that doesn't have arms – but not the sofa! You also need to sit properly when practising; it's very easy to slouch when playing, which can result in bad technique and even injury, so having a good seat is vital, as is having a music stand. These are pretty cheap and will enable you to read the exercises shown here clearly and comfortably.

When you have your practice area sorted, you then have to make the sacrifice of securing time in your daily routine to play guitar. Practice should really become habit, a daily activity. Of course, in the real world this isn't always possible, but try your hardest to make it a part of daily life. The more you play, the faster you'll improve.

Your frame of mind is also very important. Practice should be fun, something you want to do and look forward to. I've never understood guitarists who complain about practising; if you feel this way, why play the guitar? It's not compulsory! You should want to play your guitar in every situation, be it practising technique or jamming along with friends or a backing track. *All* of these activities should be fun. Getting into a positive frame of mind is a must, and will help you to achieve your goals.

OK, I think that's enough waffle. Now it's time to start the first lesson, and so, in the words of the legendary Frank Zappa, 'Shut up 'n play yer guitar.'

WEEK 1

OVERVIEW

This is it, your first week of lessons. We're going to start off by taking things nice and gently, looking at some basic techniques to get you started. Here's a list of key subjects that will be covered this week:

- Tuning the guitar and learning string names;
- Playing your first chords;
- Changing between chords;
- Basic rhythm technique;
- Learning a basic 12-bar blues progression and playing to a backing track.

Electric Guitar

DAY 1: LET'S GET STARTED!

The aim of today's lesson is to learn how to tune the guitar and how to hold the pick. We'll also look at some simple open-string picking exercises.

To start with, we need to look at how to hold the guitar. Your posture is very important, and poor posture can result in poor technique and even injury. For a start, it's important not to slouch when you're playing, and make sure you have a comfortable chair or stool that has no arms that will get in the way. You can balance the guitar on either your left or right leg, as shown in the two pictures below; this is down to personal preference. However, you must make sure that your back is straight and that your shoulders are level. Guitarists often raise the shoulders of their picking hands, but this puts the muscle to unnecessary use, resulting in tension in the picking arm.

ou should also get used to practising standing up, and very often it's the best way

practise. Just make sure your guitar strap isn't too low and your music stand is

a sensible height.

Once you're sitting (or standing) comfortably, you're ready to get in tune. One of

the most essential pieces of equipment that any guitarist can buy is an electronic

guitar tuner. These are relatively cheap to buy – although I wouldn't get one that's

too cheap, as you want it to be accurate and stable. Although you can simply use

a tuner, it's important for you to be able to tune the guitar by ear and to be able to

hear when it's out of tune, and the technique we'll be looking at here is the

relative-tuning technique. The basic concept of this approach is that the guitar is

tuned to itself.

Electric Guitar

First, let's learn the names of all six strings. The thinnest string is the first string, and is tuned to the note of E. Next is the B string, and the third string is tuned to G. With the fourth string, D, we move from the plain strings to the wound strings. The next string, the fifth, is A, and finally the sixth is the thickest, tuned to a low E. Take some time to practise playing each string and saying the name out loud.

Assuming that the sixth string – the low E – is pretty much in tune, it's now possible to tune the rest of the guitar to this string. Simply place your first fretting hand finger onto the fifth fret of the lowest string and play it with the picking hand. Let the note ring and play the fifth string (A). The note fretted on the bottom string is A – the same pitch as the open fifth string. You should be able to hear the strings are out of tune, as the sound of the unison notes will oscillate and appear to 'wobble'. If this occurs, simply raise or lower the pitch of the fifth string by turning the machine head until the oscillation stops.

Now drop the fretting-hand finger down to the fifth fret of the fifth string (A) – which is the note of D, the same pitch as the fourth string – and play both strings together, adjusting the tuning of the D string. Now place your finger on the fifth fret of the fourth string (G) and play it against the open G string, tuning where necessary, and then on the *fourth* fret of the G string (B) and play it against the second string, adjusting the latter until the notes are the same. Finally, place your finger on the fifth fret of the B string and play it against the open top string (E). Both of these notes should sound the same pitch.

xercises 1a and 1b below show this tuning technique in both tab/standard

otation and chord-box diagrams. Don't worry if this seems a little bit tricky to

tart with, and be sure to check the sound of the tuning procedure on the

ccompanying CD to help with pitching.

xercise 1a

xercise 1b

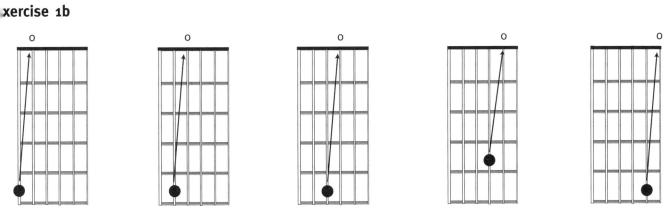

he technique of tuning is something that will develop over time as your ears

ecome more finely tuned.

Electric Guitar

Now we're going to move on to some simple open string exercises to get the picking hand working. First, let's look at how to hold the pick. I would suggest holding it with the flat of the thumb and the side of the first finger, as shown in the picture below:

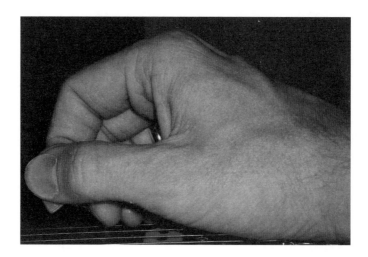

Now that you have your pick in place, it's vital that you position your right hand correctly to enable you to play the following exercises. I would suggest resting the hand on the bridge. However, take care if you have a whammy bar that floats, as too much pressure on the bridge will raise the pitches of the strings.

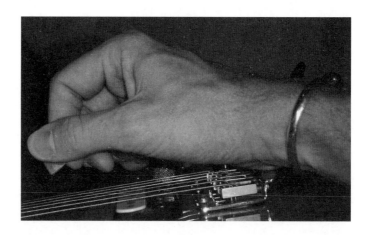

Electric Guitar

Exercise 2 is a simple exercise that moves across from the sixth string to the first,

and then back to the sixth. Try playing this exercise with all downpicks (marked ⊓):

Exercise 2

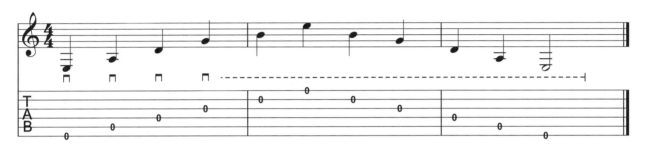

Exercise 3 is similar but jumps strings. Take care with this exercise – you don't

want to strike an unwanted string:

Exercise 3

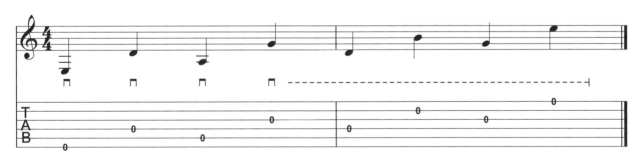

Exercise 4 is a variation on Exercise 2 and simply doubles up the open strings. When

practising this, try to use the *alternate-picking technique* – ie strike the first note

with a downstroke, then the second repeated note with an upstroke (marked ∨).

Electric Guitar

Exercise 4

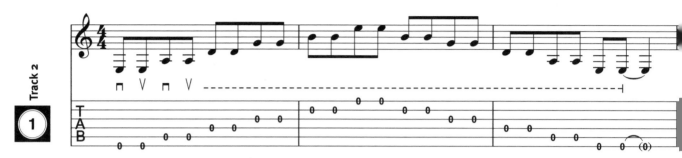

Exercise 5 is a variation on Exercise 3, jumping across the strings. To play this, use

the alternate-picking technique:

Exercise 5

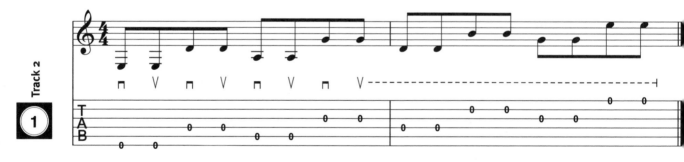

DAY 2: YOUR FIRST CHORDS

Your main task today is to learn your first three major chords. We'll also take a quick look at the position of the fretting hand and the placement of the fingers on the strings.

To enable you to play chords and single notes clearly, it's important that you position your hand correctly. The pressure should be even – don't grab the neck and press down too hard, or you'll cramp up. The picture below is a good example of the correct fretting-hand position:

Now onto holding down a note. To do this properly, place the fingertips of the fretting hand onto the desired string, next to the fretwire itself. Don't place the finger actually on the fretwire, though, or the note will sound muted and buzzy. The picture over the page demonstrates how to position your fingers when fretting a single note:

Electric Guitar

Now let's take a look at our first three chords. All of these chords are *major* chords, which means that they have a happy, bright sound. The chords we'll be looking at are A major, D major and E major.

Exercise 1 illustrates the positions of all three of these chords. To play the A chord, place your first finger on the D string (second fret), your second finger on the G string (second fret) and your third finger on the B string (second fret). The A and top E strings are left open, while the low E should not be played.

Exercise 1

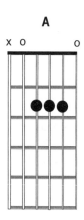

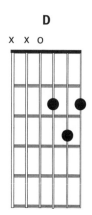

To play the D chord, place your first finger on the G string (second fret), your third finger on the B string (third fret) and your second finger on the top E string (second fret). The D string is played open and both the low E and A strings should not be played.

To play the E major chord, place your second finger on the A string (second fret), your third finger on the D string (second fret) and your first finger on the G string (first fret). The remaining strings should be played open.

When playing these chords, it's important that all of the notes are clear and aren't choked. Practise them with single downstrums.

DAY 2 STUDY

Exercise 2 is our first chord study, using all of the chords you've learned today. Simply strum each chord four times and then move on to the next. The aim here is not to stop between the chord changes, and to keep the rhythm constant. When changing, try to find fingers that share common strings between each chord – for example, the third finger uses the B string for both the A and D chords; it simply shifts up to the third fret from the second when changing from A to D. Also, the first finger remains on the G string when changing between the chords of D and E, simply dropping down one fret.

Exercise 2

Electric Guitar

Exercise 3 is a slightly more tricky study, with the chords changing every two strums. This will take a little more practice, so be patient, and remember to keep the fingers on the strings whenever possible.

Exercise 3

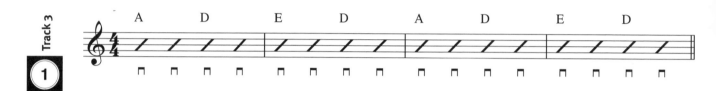

Exercise 4 uses a technique known as *chord arpeggios*. Here, each note of the chord is played separately and allowed to ring over the next. This is a great exercise for making sure that all of the notes are played cleanly.

Exercise 4

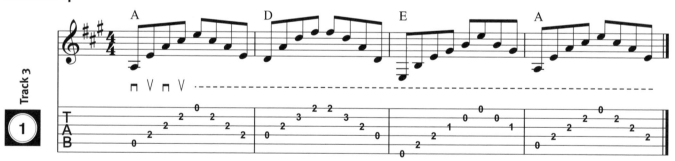

Exercise 5 is a variation on the previous example, albeit slightly more taxing. This one uses the same chord-arpeggio technique but requires you to jump across the strings, missing out every other string. You run the risk of hitting an unwanted string playing this, so take your time and be patient.

Electric Guitar

Exercise 5

Electric Guitar

DAY 3: I GOT RHYTHM...

OK, over the last couple of days we've concentrated on learning some basic chords and looked at left- and right-hand technique. Now it's time to inject a bit of rhythm into the chords and make the exercises sound more musical.

As a guitarist, you'll spend probably 90% of your time playing chords as accompaniment in a band environment, so it's vital that you understand simple rhythms and subdivisions of time. Many guitarists are more interested in flashy lead techniques than in holding down a steady groove, but you still need to spend plenty of time developing your rhythm technique. At this stage, I should point out that it would be a good idea to invest in a *metronome* – a simple piece of equipment that ticks like a clock at various speeds; it will help you develop a good sense of rhythm and build up speed when you start to learn about soloing.

To be able to play in time, it's important to understand the basics of rhythm and how you can apply this to your everyday playing.

Exercise 1 shows some basic subdivisions of time. We're looking at bars that have four beats in them, written as *4/4 time*. In this figure – known as a *time signature* – the top number determines how many beats in the bar, while the bottom number determines the length of each beat. (This will be discussed further on in the book, so don't worry about it for now.)

The first note value we're going to look at is a *whole note*, which lasts for four beats.

Simply play a note on the first beat and count, 'One, two, three, four.' If we cut this note in half we get two *half notes*, which last for two beats each. Play the first note on beat 1 and let it ring for beat 2, then play the next note on beat 3 and let it ring for beat 4. Cut these two notes in half and we get four *quarter notes*, each lasting for one beat. Simply play a note on each beat, counting evenly, 'One, two, three, four.'

Finally, if we cut our four quarter notes in half we get eight *eighth notes*. For this rhythmic value, we have to play two notes per beat. The second note of each beat appears on the off beat, or the 'and'. When practising this, simply count and play evenly – 'One and two and three and four and.' Try using an upstroke on the 'and'.

Exercise 1

In standard music notation, these rhythm symbols are used to let the musician know how long certain notes in a melody should last. But what if you were just reading a chord rhythm chart? In standard guitar-music notation, the noteheads are replaced with diagonal slashes that symbolise strum patterns.

Exercise 2 shows the note values of the previous example with the noteheads replaced by rhythm slashes. Make sure you listen to the CD and count along with the click to hear how long each strum lasts:

Electric Guitar

Exercise 2

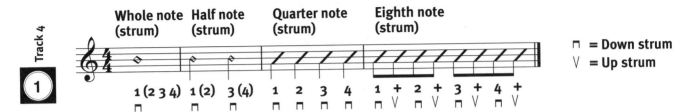

Exercise 3 will help you to practise our three chords in a sequence based on a quarter-note rhythm. Try to remember how to change chords from the previous day's lesson:

Exercise 3

Exercise 4 contains the same progression found in the previous example, but the rhythm has been changed to an eighth-note rhythm. (Notice how an upward strum is used on the 'and' of the beat...) Remember to keep everything nice and even:

Exercise 4

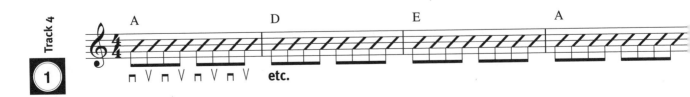

DAY 3 STUDY

Exercise 5 is today's final example and is a short study piece. This example requires you to practise our three chords in a short melodic progression using an eighth-note rhythm. Aim to execute smooth changes between the chords, and aim for a steady, even rhythmic pattern:

Exercise 5

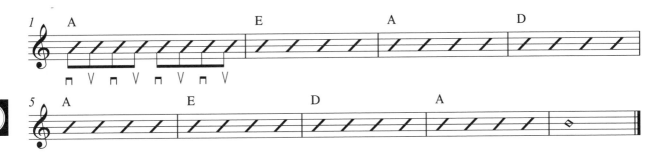

Track 4

1

45

Electric Guitar

DAY 4: CHORD EXTENSIONS

In today's lesson we're going to look at some simple extensions of the major chords we've learned so far. We'll also look at practising these chords in a sequence and as chord arpeggios.

Exercise 1 shows three new chords: A7, D7, and E7. Hopefully, you should be fairly familiar with reading chord diagrams by now, but if you get a little lost, listen to the sound of each of these chords on the CD:

Exercise 1

A chord extension is a simple way of adding variation and spicing up the chords you already use. All it involves is simply adding an extra note to the chords from the scale of the same name. Too much theory? Don't panic – we'll cover this in more detail later on. All you have to worry about for now is remembering these three variations. You'll notice that, with a small change in its shape, the sound of the chord changes dramatically. The seventh – actually the *dominant seventh* – chord has a very bluesy sound.

Exercise 2 is a short progression that uses the quarter-note strumming pattern from Exercise 2, Day 3. Use it to help you change between the chord shapes. This exercise also includes a new symbol, ⅍, which means you have to repeat the previous bar. The diagonal slashes mean continue with the existing strum pattern.

Exercise 2

Exercise 3 is a slight variation on the previous example and makes use of the eighth-note rhythm from Exercise 4, Day 3. Make sure you stick to that strict alternating up-and-down strumming pattern, and make sure you keep things sounding nice and even:

Exercise 3

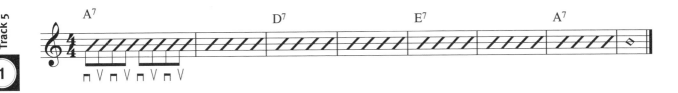

Exercise 4 includes some pretty quick changes, with two chords in each bar:

Electric Guitar

Exercise 4

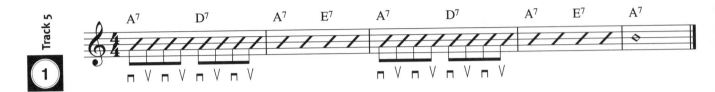

Exercise 5 harks back to the chord-arpeggio approach and shifts through all three
of our new chords. This type of practice is an excellent way of making sure that all
of the notes of the chords are clean and clear:

Exercise 5

Exercise 6 is our final example for today and uses more chord-arpeggio sequences.
This example skips across the strings and uses all three of our new shapes. It's a
great exercise for improving the accuracy of the picking hand, as well as making
sure the chords are played cleanly:

Electric Guitar

Exercise 6

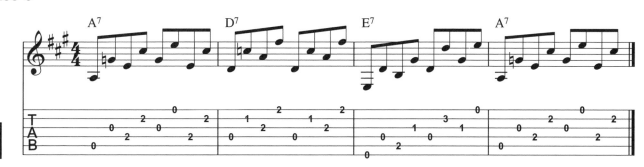

Track 5

1

Electric Guitar

DAY 5: RHYTHMS, RESTS AND MUSIC SHORTHAND

We've got a lot to get through today, as not only are we going to work on changing major chords to dominant seventh chords but we're also going to learn a little about music shorthand.

So far, I've told you how long to play each note. But what about how long *not* to play? Rests – the gaps between notes – are as important as the notes themselves. Indeed many styles, such as funk and reggae, rely heavily on rests.

Exercise 1 shows the rest value for each of the rhythms we've looked at so far:

Exercise 1

Whole note rest	Half note rest	Quarter note rest	Eighth note rest

Obviously I can't get you to practise this bar as it's written, but it's very important that you remember these symbols as they will be used in examples later in this book.

Exercise 2 contains some symbols that are vital when reading a rhythm chart or a piece of music. With some songs, if they were written out literally, each would take up many sheets of paper. This, of course, is very impractical, especially if you're on

a gig and you have to leaf through a whole sheaf of papers onstage. The way around this is to use a form of musical shorthand to direct you around a piece of music.

The first example is the double barline, which marks the end of a piece (or section) of music. The next is a double barline with two dots, which means you must repeat the section between these two sets of barlines. Next is a symbol we saw earlier which tells you to repeat the previous bar. The final example is written across a barline and tells you to repeat the two previous bars. I've also included some common symbols for different time signatures: 4/4 (four quarter notes in a bar), 3/4 (three quarter notes in a bar) and finally 2/4 (two quarter notes to a bar):

Exercise 2

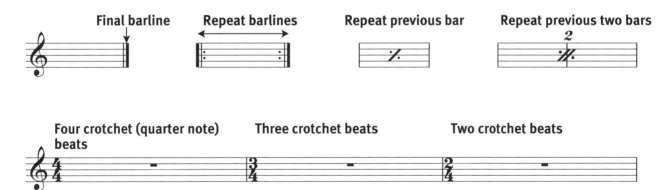

Now we're going to move on to today's practical exercises. Exercise 3 includes a simple study piece that swaps between the major chords and their dominant seventh extensions. This exercise uses a simple quarter-note rhythm and is a great way for you to hear the difference between the two chord types:

Electric Guitar

Exercise 3

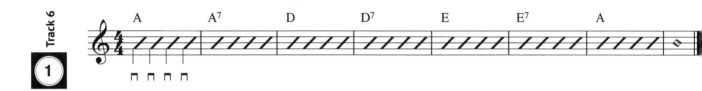

Exercise 4 contains the same progression as the previous example but in an eighth-note rhythm. Remember to keep the alternate strums nice and even:

Exercise 4

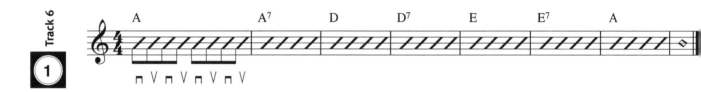

Exercise 5 uses the same progression but adds quite a bit of interest to the rhythm sound by mixing up one quarter note with six eighth notes. Make sure you pay attention to the strumming directions – a single downstrum on beat 1 followed by a down-/upstrum on the remaining beats:

Exercise 5

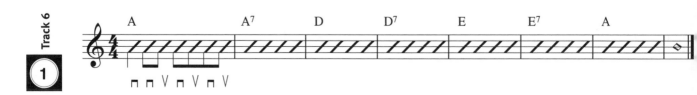

Exercise 6 is yet another variation on the same progression, this time mixing up quarter notes on beats 1 and 3 and eighth notes on 2 and 4. Once again, pay attention to the direction of your strumming pattern:

Exercise 6

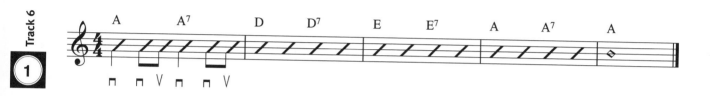

Electric Guitar

DAY 6: TAB AND MORE CHORDS

OK, we've come this far without any real lessons in reading music, but as I said in the 'Reading Music' section earlier, the aim of this book is to teach guitar, not sight-reading. To kick things off, we're going to look at how to read tab, the most common guitar notation. We'll also look at two new major chords.

The tab stave is made up of six lines (as opposed to the five lines of the traditional music stave) representing the six strings of the guitar. The bottom line is the sixth string (low E) and the top line is the first string (high E). The numbers written on the lines represent the frets at which these strings should be played. Open strings are marked with a zero.

Exercise 1 gives an example of a simple tab melody, based around the C major scale, performed on the A and D strings. Have a go at the exercise and then listen to the CD to see if you got it right:

Exercise 1

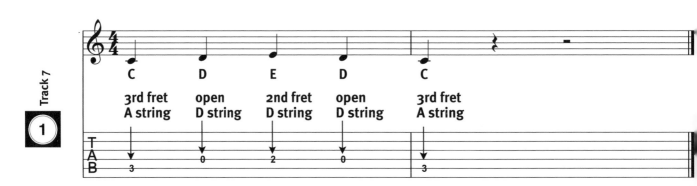

Electric Guitar

ab can also be used to write chords. When two or more notes are to be played

ogether, the tab numbers are stacked on top of each other. Exercise 2

emonstrates some simple chords. Once again, play each one and then play the

D example to check if they sound the same:

xercise 2

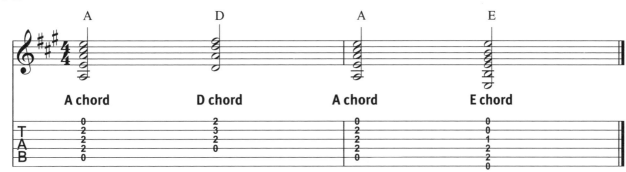

xercise 3 includes an idea where the chord is separated by single notes taken

rom the chord. This sort of strumming pattern is used by many country guitarists:

xercise 3

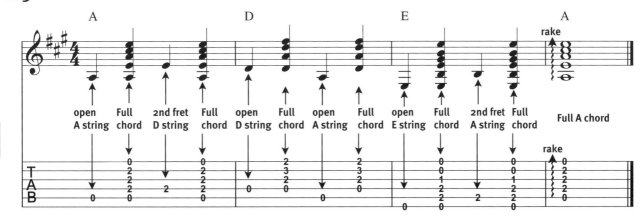

Electric Guitar

Now it's time for some new chords. Exercise 4 includes two new major chords: C major and G major. These chords are quite tricky and require some stretching, but even so, make sure each note is nice and clean and clear:

Exercise 4

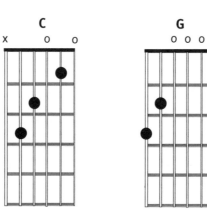

Now we've taken a look at these new chords, it's time to put them together with some of the other chords. Exercise 5 uses the chords of C major, G major and major. As the new chords are quite tricky, this exercise might take a bit of practice but try not to lose patience. Also, pay attention to the rhythmic pattern, which features more mixtures of quarter notes and eighth notes:

Exercise 5

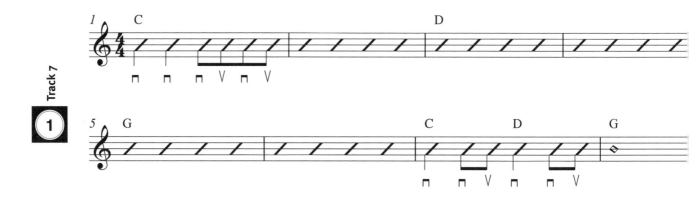

Electric Guitar

Exercise 6 is even trickier and uses more of the chords we've looked at so far. There are lots of awkward changes in this progression, so take your time. Also, look out for the rhythmic pattern:

Exercise 6

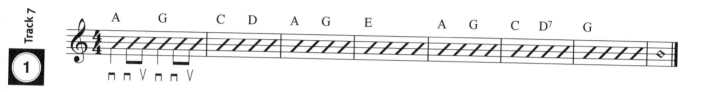

Exercise 7 is a chord-arpeggio sequence based on C and G major. This exercise is designed to get you playing all of the chord notes nice and cleanly:

Exercise 7

Exercise 8 is our final example of the day and uses our old friend, the string-jumping arpeggio. In this one, not only do you have to concentrate on the new chord stretches, but you have to jump strings when performing the arpeggio. Ouch!

Electric Guitar

Exercise 8

DAY 7

WEEK 1 TEST

Congratulations! You made it through your first week. You should now have enough information under your belt to tackle Week 2. Just to make sure that everything is sinking in, here are a few short questions:

1 What are the names of the open strings of the guitar?

2 What type of sound does a major chord have?

3 How do you write an open string on guitar tab?

4 How long does a whole note last?

5 How should you hold the pick, and where should you position the picking hand?

Electric Guitar

Now that short test is out of the way, it's time for a reward. This week you've learned eight new chords, and we've taken a look at some rhythmic variations and ways in which we can change between chords. We've also looked at some music shorthand to help us navigate around a rhythm chart. Our first end-of-week study piece is a simple 12-bar blues that uses the chords of A major, D major, E major, A7, D7, and E7.

The blues is a very common type of progression which is still very popular. This type of progression is referred to as a 'I–IV–V', and as a budding guitarist it's important that you know how to play one. Actually, this track possibly won't sound that bluesy to start with, as this is the blues in its most basic form – and, after all, you've been playing for only seven days! But give it time; this simple progression will eventually develop into something very special. First, jam along with the full track, and when you're feeling confident, skip to the CD backing track, which has the guitar missing.

When you've got it down, why not get the family in for a special performance so they can all hear the results of your first week's efforts? Performing to an audience, no matter how small, is a great way of building confidence. Good luck!

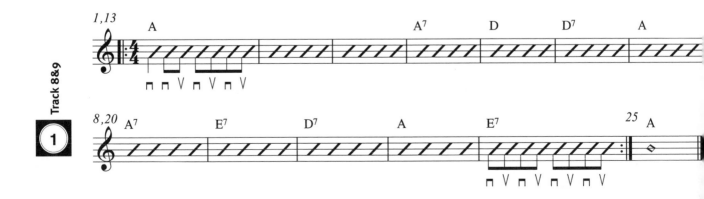

WEEK 2

OVERVIEW

Well, you made it through the first week. Hopefully your fingers aren't too sore. Just try to remember that all the pain and suffering will be worth it. I also hope you're sticking to an organised and regular practice routine. After all, you didn't clear out that practice room for nothing!

Anyway, lets take a look at what you'll be doing this week:

- Learning more new chords;
- Learning how to play your first single note blues riff;
- Working on alternate picking;
- Learning a swing blues.

Electric Guitar

DAY 8: MORE SEVENTH CHORDS AND PROGRESSIONS

Last week you learned five major and three dominant seventh chords. We're going to start off this week with two more seventh chords.

Exercise 1 includes the chords of C7, and G7. Both chords are a little troublesome, the C7 chord using all four fingers, while the G7 includes an awkward stretch. Make sure you practise these chords using the chord arpeggios from last week's chord examples.

QUOTE FOR THE WEEK

The acoustic guitar is a horrid little box. It doesn't sing... But the electric? You can make it do anything.

– *Pete Townshend, The Who*

Exercise 1

Track 10

1

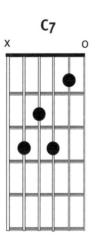

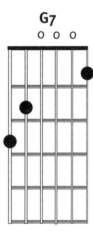

Now let's move on to some practice progressions. Exercise 2 swaps between the chords of G/G7 and C/C7. The change between these chords will require a lot of left-hand accuracy, so practise this exercise *slowly*. This progression also includes one of the rhythmic variations we looked at last week:

Electric Guitar

Exercise 2

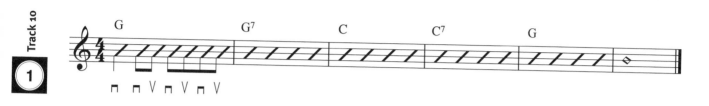

Exercise 3 combines some of last week's dominant seventh chords with today's

chords. Again, some of these moves are quite tricky, so take care:

Exercise 3

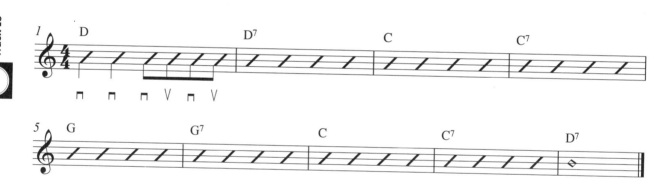

Exercise 4 is the last progression for today. Watch out for the G7 – it's a pretty

awkward change:

Exercise 4

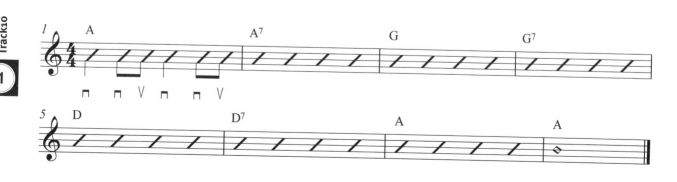

Electric Guitar

! All of these rhythm studies use a mixture of quarter-note and eighth-note rhythmic patterns. Remember, as a guitarist you'll be spending a lot of your time playing chords, so having a tight and accurate rhythm technique is essential. To my mind, the two most important factors of playing guitar are to play both in tune and in time. It doesn't matter how technically well or how fast you can play; if it's not in time and tuneful, what's the point? So make sure you spend time with the rhythm studies shown here. Oh, and have you got that metronome yet?

To finish off today's lesson, we're going to look at two simple finger exercises. These are aimed at getting your left and right hands synchronised, building up stamina and getting them up to speed. (Incidentally, these exercises aren't meant to be musical, but purely mechanical, so ignore any comments from other members of your house. They won't be complaining when you're blasting like Gary Moore!)

Exercise 5 is a simple exercise that uses a two-fret stretch across all six strings. You should play this exercise with a steady eighth-note rhythm and strict alternate picking. Make sure you keep the picking hand relaxed, and try to keep things clean:

Exercise 5

Exercise 6 is simply the descending version of the previous exercise. Descending

patterns are often easier, so don't rush on the way back down:

Exercise 6

Electric Guitar

DAY 9: SWING RHYTHMS AND MORE PICKING

Like I said at the end of last week, the blues is a very common chord progression for guitarists to play when they first start, but the blues you saw a few pages back was very simple – well, it was only Week 1! The main thing that was missing was the swing rhythm, which displaces the upbeat, or the 'and', making it fall slightly late.

Exercise 1a is a normal bar of eighth notes, with two eighth notes to each beat:

Exercise 1a

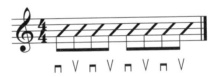

Exercise 1b has a new rhythm. They're still eighth notes, but there are three of them to a beat, grouped together, with a '3' marked over the top. These are *eighth-note triplets* – ie three eighth notes played in the time you'd normally play two. The best way to count them is to break them down into syllables. Try counting 'one-trip-let, two-trip-let, three-trip-let, four-trip-let'. If you say the three syllables evenly on each beat, you'll count a triplet rhythm.

Exercise 1b

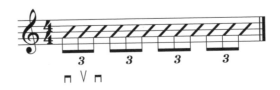

Exercise 1c includes yet another variation, demonstrating how a swing rhythm is written. You'll notice that the first two eighth notes of the triplet have been swapped with one quarter note, which results in the uneven, displaced rhythm I mentioned earlier. This is known as a *broken triplet*:

Exercise 1c

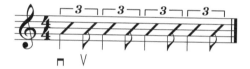

Even though Exercise 1c illustrates the correct way a swing rhythm should be written, it looks pretty messy. If a piece is to be played with a swing feel, it's written as shown below in Exercise 1d. You'll notice that above Exercise 1d there's a symbol comprising two eighth notes, an 'equals' symbol and then the broken-triplet symbol. This means that all eighth notes are to be played as broken triplets. Simple!

Exercise 1d

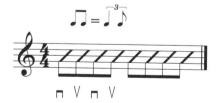

Electric Guitar

Exercise 2 is today's study piece and uses the new broken-triplet/swing rhythm.

Playing the dominant-seventh chords with the new rhythm gives the progression a

really bluesy edge.

Exercise 2

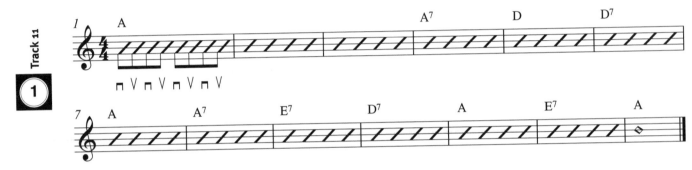

Exercise 3 is a picking/finger exercise that uses three notes per string, so take

things nice and slowly:

Exercise 3

Exercise 4 is the descending version of the previous example. Once again, keep

things even and don't rush on the way down.

Electric Guitar

Exercise 4

Electric Guitar

DAY 10: ENTER THE POWER CHORD!

Today we're going to look at the *power chord*, an essential tool when playing rock guitar. The chord itself is made up of only two notes, and as a result is neither major nor minor and will work over both tonalities.

OK, let's talk a little about chord theory. All regular chords start their lives as *triads*, meaning that they comprise just three notes: the first, third and fifth notes of the scale of the same name. Therefore, to change a major chord into a minor chord, simply lower the third by a *semitone* (ie one fret) to turn it into a minor third.

The power chord is made up of only the first and fifth notes of the scale. The first is often referred to as the *tonic* or *root note* – ie the note that gives the chord (and scale) its name. Because they have no third, power chords have a very tight and punchy sound, hence the name. They also work great with a crunch tone.

Exercise 1 illustrates the open-position power chords of A5, D5, and E5. Try cranking the gain a little on your amp when you try them out:

Exercise 1

Now let's try these chords with a rhythmic pattern. Because they cover only two strings, the strum pattern needs to be more concentrated, so the next few exercises require you to play only downstrums, which helps to drive rhythm parts and have a great rock sound.

Exercises 2, 3 and 4 illustrate rhythm studies that use the chords of A5, D5 and E5, respectively. Try to cut down on the movement of the picking hand and isolate it to just the two strings required:

Exercise 2

Exercise 3

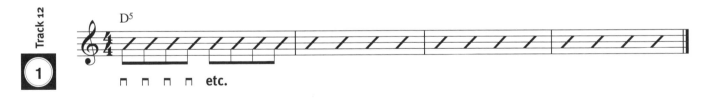

Exercise 4

Electric Guitar

Now you've practised the downstrum rhythm, we're going to have a look at a new technique called *palm-muting*. The basic idea of palm-muting is that you rest the fleshy part of your picking-hand palm on the edge of the strings at the bridge. This has the effect of muting the sound. The picture below will give you an idea of how your hand should sit:

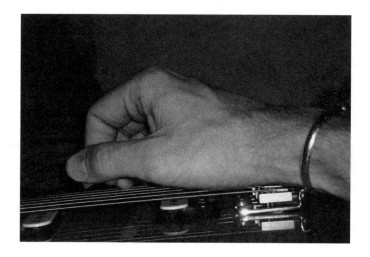

Now try the playing the A5 chord in Exercise 5 and listen to the difference palm-muting makes. You should also try this with the other power chords you've learnt:

Exercise 5

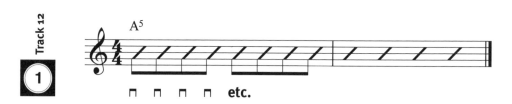

OK, one last variation. Now it's time to add some life into our muted rhythm pattern by adding some accents (marked $>$). To do this, simply remove the palm

muting to make the riff really jump out. Exercise 6a and Exercise 6b give two examples of accented rhythms.

Exercise 6a

Exercise 6b

To finish off today's studies, I've included two four-note-per-string chromatic patterns. Exercise 7 includes the ascending pattern while Exercise 8 is the descending pattern. This type of exercise can be included in your practice routine for many years, so I would suggest making a note of the tempo every time you practise to gauge your improvement.

Electric Guitar

Exercise 7

Exercise 8

DAY 11: BLUES RIFFS

Now we're really starting to get somewhere. Hopefully things are starting to sound

a little more like the guitar sounds in your head. Today we're going to take things a

little further and help you take your first steps towards playing lead guitar. To kick

things off, we'll be putting our riff and swing rhythm into a study piece.

DAY 11 STUDY PIECE

Exercise 1 includes our three new power chords plus our swing rhythm, all

performed with downstrokes. Be sure to pay special attention to the repeat bars.

This piece should sound more like a real blues progression:

Exercise 1

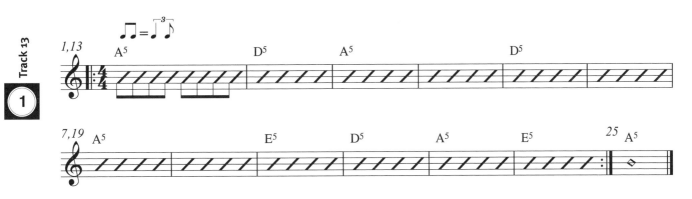

Electric Guitar

Now it's time to put our single-note studies into practice. However, instead of being chromatic (ie based on a series of semitones), the next few exercises are based on a single-note riff, written around the chords of A7, D7, and E7, each riff serving to outline the notes from the chord it implies. All of the examples use an eighth-note swing rhythm and should be played with alternate picking.

Exercise 2 outlines the A7 chords and starts from the A, the chord's root note:

Exercise 2

Exercise 3 outlines the D7 chords, starting from the root:

Exercise 3

Exercise 4 is the final riff today and is based around the E5 chord, starting from the root:

Exercise 4

It's possible to transpose these riffs into other keys simply by shifting the root to the note of the desired key, keeping the riff formula the same. Why not try going back to the study piece you learnt on Day 7 and replacing those chords with the riffs shown here?

This type of riff is very common in blues and is an essential style when learning the electric guitar. Indeed, riffs like this one can be heard on many Jimmy Page tracks. Make sure you keep the picking and timing consistent, though, and practise the riffs with a metronome first.

Electric Guitar

DAY 12: MORE RIFFS

Now we're going to look at some new riff ideas, this time based on chords. Artists such as Aerosmith, Status Quo and Stevie Ray Vaughan have used the following style of riffs, so you can see that they're very versatile.

Exercise 1 is a variation on the power chord and demonstrates how, simply by moving the fifth up one note at a time, we get some new chords. The first thing to understand is that on all of our power chords the lower note of the pair is the root note and the note on the adjacent string is the fifth. If we move the fifth up a tone (ie two frets) we get a sixth, resulting in a *sixth chord*. If we move the sixth up a semitone (ie one fret), we get a *flat seventh*, resulting in a *dominant seventh chord*.

The riff in Exercise 1 includes the chords of A5, A6 and A7. Try this riff with the downstroke rhythm we looked at earlier. Also, try adding a little crunch to your sound.

Exercise 1

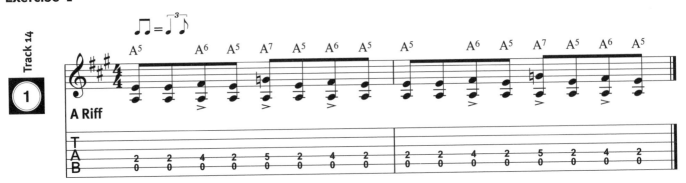

Exercise 2 includes the same alterations to the D5 chord and results in the chords of D6 and D7:

Exercise 2

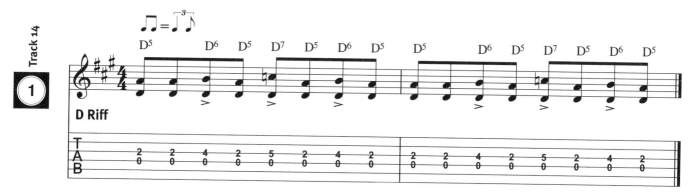

Exercise 3 includes the same alterations to the chord of E5, giving us E6 and E7.

(Note that all of the riffs shown here include the swing rhythm.)

Exercise 3

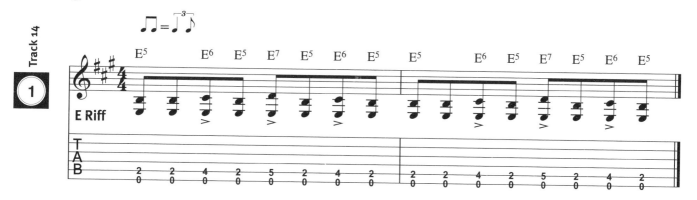

To make things a little easier for those still struggling with tab, Exercises 4, 5 and

6 include all of our new chords as fret diagrams:

Electric Guitar

Exercise 4

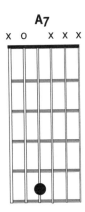

Exercise 5

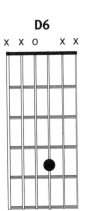

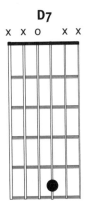

Exercise 6

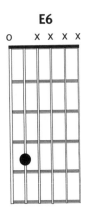

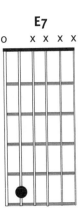

Just to show you how easy it is to come up with riffs, I've embellished a little on the single-note riffs you learnt yesterday simply by mixing up the notes of the original riff, but still starting from the root. Exercises 7, 8 and 9 include new a riff built around A7, D7 and E7, respectively. Again, look out for the swing rhythm again to keep things nice and bluesy:

Exercise 7

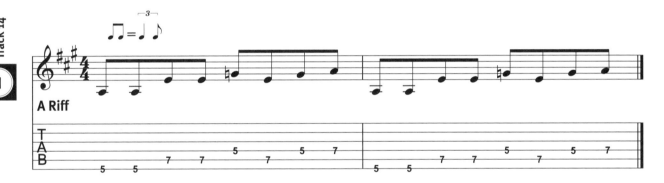

Exercise 8

Electric Guitar

Exercise 9

DAY 12 STUDY PIECE

Exercise 10 includes a rhythm chart for a swing blues in A. Where there should be

chord names, you'll see the terms 'A riff', 'D riff' and 'E riff'. All you have to do here

is play the relevant riff over each chord. The piece repeats, allowing you to have a

go at the both of the riffs you learned today.

Exercise 10

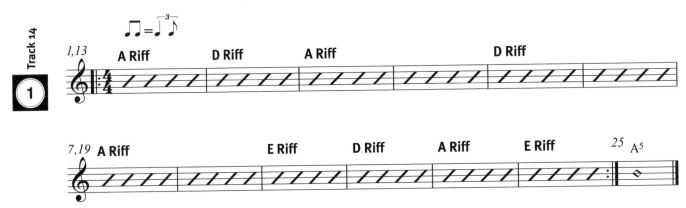

DAY 13: ADDING THIRDS TO OUR RIFFS

Today we're going to look at yet more variations on our single-note riffs. First, we're going to add the major third to all three to give the riffs a definite major feel. (Previously, none of the riffs included a third, allowing them to work over either major or minor chords.) I've also included a vital tool when writing riffs and melodies: the question–answer technique.

You'll notice that the riffs are now two bars in length. This is because they include two complementary sections, the first asking the question and the second answering. When you listen to many blues records, the guitar often answers vocal lines with licks, giving the listener the illusion of the vocalist and guitarist having a musical conversation. This is a very effective tool when trying to come up with memorable melodies and catchy riffs.

Exercises 1, 2 and 3 contain our new question–answer riffs, based around the chords of A7, D7 and E7, respectively:

Exercise 1

Electric Guitar

Exercise 2

Exercise 3

DAY 13 STUDY PIECE

To round things off, I've given you a new blues rhythm chart in the key of A. Once again, the word 'riff' appears after each chord name, so it's up to you to add the appropriate riff over the correct chord. Why not try coming up with some of your own riffs?

Exercise 4

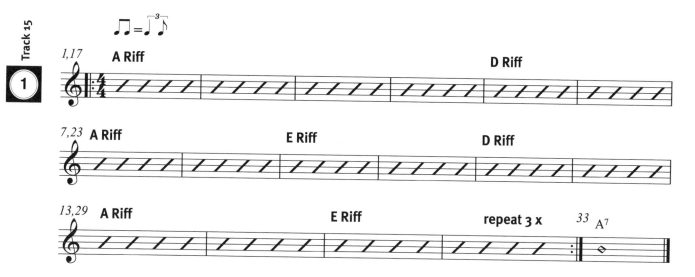

Electric Guitar

DAY 14

 WEEK 2 TEST

It's that time of the week again, so before you have some fun with this week's jam track, here are a few simple questions to answer, just to see how you're getting on.

1 How many notes in a power chord?

2 Why will power chords work over both major and minor chords?

3 What do you call a group of three eighth notes on one quarter-note beat?

4 What symbol tells you to swing an eighth-note rhythm?

5 What note must you move, and by how far, to turn a power chord into a sixth chord?

Electric Guitar

WEEK 2 STUDY PIECE

Now for the good part, a bit of fun after all your hard efforts. Here's a cool swing-blues progression that uses all of the chords and riffs you've learnt so far. The first 12 bars are based on normal open major and dominant seventh chords, and the next 12 bars feature power chords with sixth and seventh chord extensions. The final 12 bars include some single-note riffs. Take care of the stabs at the end of the track, and pay attention to the eighth-note rest in bar 37. For the riff sections, try adding some crunch to your sound. When you've learnt the piece in full, try coming up with your own riffs and arrangements.

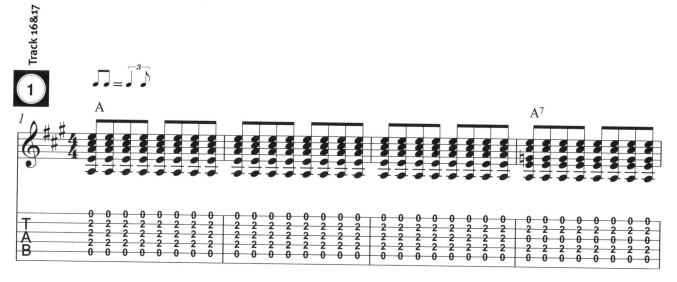

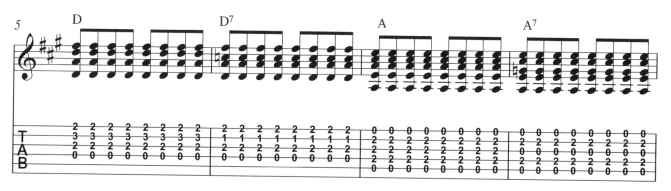

continues...

Electric Guitar

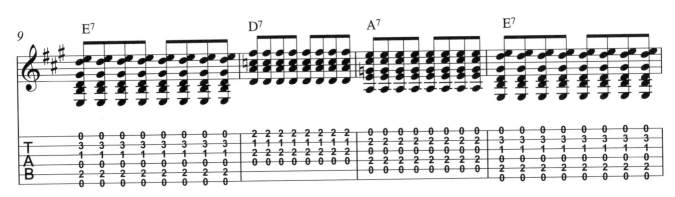

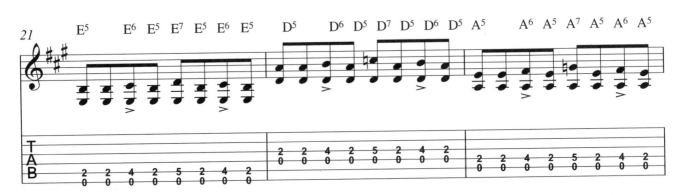

Electric Guitar

WEEK 3

OVERVIEW

Welcome to Week 3. Hopefully you're remembering your chords and have started to experiment with some blues riff ideas of your own. Try not to get complacent about your practice, though, and remember that it's important to stick to a routine. It doesn't take much to get out of sync, so be strict with yourself.

Let's take a look at this week's main objectives:

- To learn minor and minor seventh chords;
- To learn new rhythms, and ties;
- To learn new music shorthand;
- To learn extended finger exercises.

Electric Guitar

DAY 15: MINOR CHORDS

We're going to start off this week by adding some new chords to your growing vocabulary. So far we've learned five major and dominant seventh shapes, and to kick off proceedings we'll be taking a look at our first three minor chords.

QUOTE FOR THE WEEK

I started taking piano lessons when I was really young, but about a year later I saw a guitar at a yard sale and thought it was much hipper!

– Richie Kotzen

As I mentioned last week, all major chords are triads; they're constructed from three notes – the first, third and fifth – taken from the major scale of the same name. If we look at the C major scale, we can see which notes are used to construct the chord:

C Major Scale

```
C D E F G A B C
1 2 3 4 5 6 7 1
```

C Major Chord

```
C E G
1 3 5
```

These notes are doubled to form a full chord voicing. Forming a minor chord, meanwhile, is very straightforward – we take the major triad and change just one note, the major third, which is lowered to E♭, the minor third, to create a minor chord.

Exercise 1 illustrates the chords of A minor, D minor and E minor:

Electric Guitar

Exercise 1

Track 18

1

Exercise 2 includes a short A minor chord sequence. Practise this with some of the

rhythmic pattern from previous exercises:

Exercise 2

Track 18

1

Exercise 3 includes the chord of D minor. Once again, use the rhythmic patterns

you learned in previous lessons, and make sure the chord sounds clean:

Exercise 3

Track 18

1

Electric Guitar

Exercise 4 is based on a chord of E minor. Again, use some of rhythms we looked at earlier, and make sure all of the notes of the chord are clean and clear:

Exercise 4

Exercises 5, 6 and 7 include the chords of A minor, D minor and E minor played as chord arpeggios. This type of exercise is a really good way of making sure you're playing all the notes of the chord cleanly:

Exercise 5

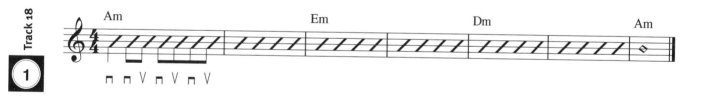

Exercise 6

Electric Guitar

Exercise 7

Exercise 8 is our final exercise for today and includes a short chord study that links our new chords together with a rhythmic pattern. Remember to find the easiest way to change from one chord to the next by looking for similarities in shapes and points where shapes share fingers on the same strings.

Exercise 8

DAY 16: MUSIC SHORTCUTS

I've already mentioned that, very often when reading a piece of music, the score isn't written out literally at length, as this wouldn't be practical. Most songs use the same verse/chorus progression and often repeat small sections. To avoid having a six-foot-long piece of music, there are symbols that are used to direct you to specific parts of the music, which means that the score can be abbreviated.

Exercise 1 illustrates the use of *first-* and *second-time bars*. The first time you play the sequence, play the G–G7 bar with the '1' over the top and then go back to the beginning of the sequence. This time around, though, you have to omit the first-time bar and jump straight to the second-time bar, which includes the chords of C major, A minor and then the final bar of C major:

Exercise 1

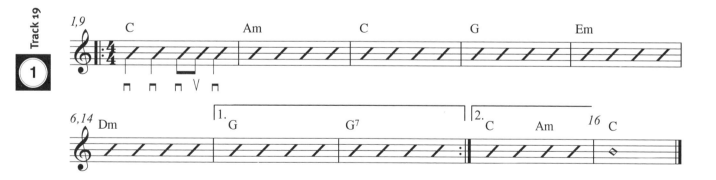

Exercise 2 is another example of the first- and second-time bar. This time I've used a different rhythm, so watch out for those accents!

Electric Guitar

Exercise 2

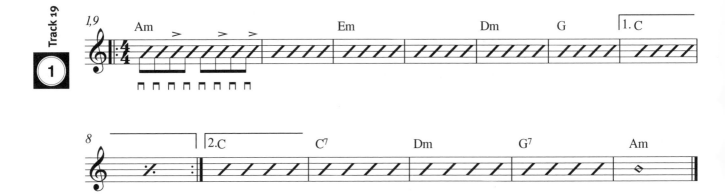

96

Electric Guitar

Exercise 2

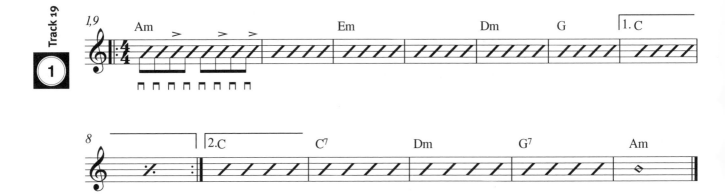

Electric Guitar

DAY 17: INTRODUCING THE TIE

Today we're going to continue with our rhythm studies and look at a new technique: the *tied rhythm*. The tie basically ties notes/rhythms together. Notes that are tied aren't re-strummed but are left to sustain. This technique can add a totally new sound to the rhythms you've learned so far, especially when the tie crosses the barline, which gives the rhythm a pushing feel.

Exercises 1–5 include different variations on the tied rhythm, and there are plenty here for you to experiment with! Make sure you listen to the CD, though, so you know exactly what's going on. One thing to remember about the tie is that you should keep the rhythm constant; if a tie falls on a down- or upstrum, for instance, execute the strum as normal. This will keep you in time and will also make sure that your hand's going in the right direction for the next strum, as you don't want to be playing a downstrum on an upbeat, and vice versa.

Exercise 1

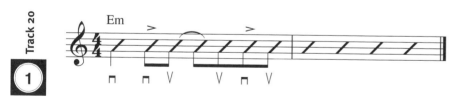

Exercise 2

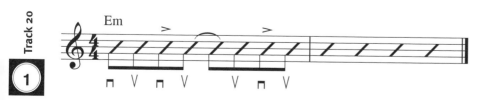

Electric Guitar

Exercise 3

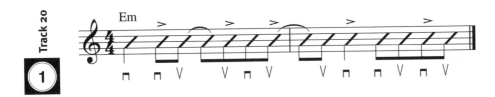

Exercise 4

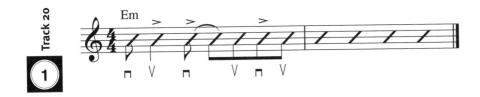

Exercise 5

X = mute strings with fretting hand

Once you've practised these exercises, it's important that you take the chords you've learnt, put them into sequences and experiment with tie variations of your own. One of the best ways to improve as a guitarist is to embellish on ideas and studies so that they really sink in. I should also stress the importance of using a metronome, as obtaining a solid rhythm technique is vital if you want to be guitarists. As I said earlier, most of your time will be spent holding down grooves, so make timekeeping an integral part of your practice.

DAY 18: THE MINOR SEVENTH CHORD

You've already learned how to extend major chords into dominant seventh chords, and how simply changing a note will drastically change the sound of your progressions. In today's lesson you'll be learning a very important chord: the *minor seventh*.

To build your own minor seventh chord, simply take a minor triad – comprising first, flat third and fifth – and add the seventh degree of the major scale. Before you add, though, first it needs to be lowered in pitch by one fret (ie semitone) to turn it into a minor seventh. If this was an A minor chord, you'd take the major seventh of A (G♯) and lower it to a G♮ (natural), giving you the notes A, C, E and G, and the formula of first, flat third, fifth and flat seventh. This chord has a great sound and will really spice up minor progressions.

Exercise 1 includes the chords of Am7, Dm7 and Em7. Make sure that all of the notes of each chord are clean and clear.

Exercise 1

Am7

Dm7

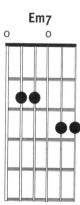
Em7

Electric Guitar

Exercise 2 is a great example of how much the sound will change when you shift from a straight minor chord to a minor seventh. This exercise uses all of the minor and minor seventh chords we've looked at so far:

Exercise 2

Well there, I bet you were thinking I was letting you off lightly today with just chords. How wrong you were! You still need to keep those fingers moving, as well as work on your picking hand. To this end, Exercise 3 elaborates on our four-note-per-string chromatic exercise by featuring a position shift up one fret. Also, the sequence is reversed on the descending leg of the pattern.

This exercise might cause you a few problems when shifting and reversing the pattern, so take your time to get to grips with it. Make sure you're playing accurately, and don't cut corners. Again, this type of exercise can be made part of your practice routine for many years to come, and it's a good idea to jot down how fast you play it each time so you can gauge how much you've improved:

Electric Guitar

Exercise 3

DAY 19: MORE COOL CHORDS

Today we're going to look at some new chords, including more major chords and
variations, plus the add9 and sus4 chord extensions.

Exercise 1 includes the chords of Cadd9, Dsus4, F and G major, but let's look at the
majors first, and our first barre (ie a fully movable chord) – in this case, a partial barre.
The barre technique is when you use the flat of your finger to hold down several strings
at once. For this version of the F major chord, you need to hold the top E and B at the
first fret. Before playing, just practise holding the barre. Try to use the outer edge of the
first finger, and make sure the notes are clear before adding the other fingers.

Although you've already learnt the chord of G major, I am giving you a new variation,
which now includes the third fret of the B string. This chord is still G major but uses
a different voicing. A voicing is simply the order in which the first, third and fifth are
stacked to make up the chord.

Next is the Cadd9, a great sounding chord. For this you simply add the ninth note of the C major scale – ie the note of D – to the C triad. (The ninth is the same as the second, but played one octave higher. This is known as a *compound interval*.)

Our last chord is a Dsus4, or D suspended fourth. For this chord you simply raise the third degree of the scale of D, the F♯, up to the fourth, G. The term 'suspended' here refers to the way the chord sounds like it's hanging, waiting to resolve to D major.

Exercise 1

Track 22

1

C add9

x   o

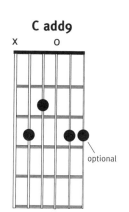

optional

D sus4

x   x   o

F

x   x

DAY 19 STUDY PIECE

Exercise 2 is our final example for the day and is a study piece that uses all of today's new chords plus some previous ones. The exercise comprises chord arpeggios, so you can check you're playing all of the chord notes cleanly.

Electric Guitar

Exercise 2

DAY 20: MORE TERMS AND SIGNS

As we've looked at quite a few chords over the last few days, today we'll take a break

from them and have a look at some new signs: the *DS* sign and the *coda*. The DS (*dal*

segno – literally 'from the sign') is used to direct you back to a specific point in a piece

of music (marked by a 𝄋 sign) and is useful in reducing repetition of sections on a

score, and the coda (literally 'tail', marked ⊕) is the end section of a piece of music.

Exercise 1 includes a short progression that uses the DS sign. When you reach the

DS, jump back to where we see the 𝄋 sign, above the F chord, then start playing

again from that point:

Exercise 1

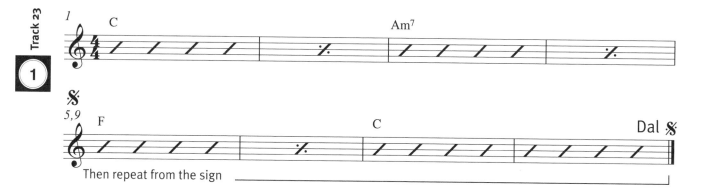

Exercise 2 includes both a DS and a Coda. Play up to the DS and go back to the 𝄋

sign over the Am7 bar, then play up to the ⊕ sign and jump straight to the coda

section, which that starts with the Dm7 chord:

Electric Guitar

Exercise 2

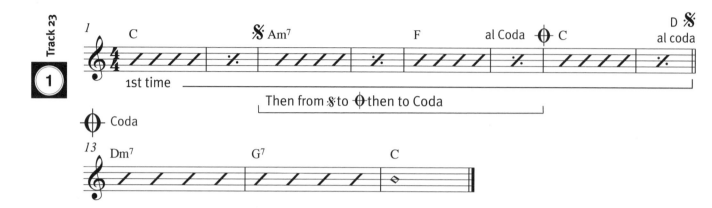

DAY 20 STUDY PIECE

Exercise 3 is today's study piece, and it mixes up arpeggiating part of the chord with a rhythmic pattern. This style of rhythm playing is an excellent way of breaking up your rhythm technique and adding some dynamics:

Exercise 3

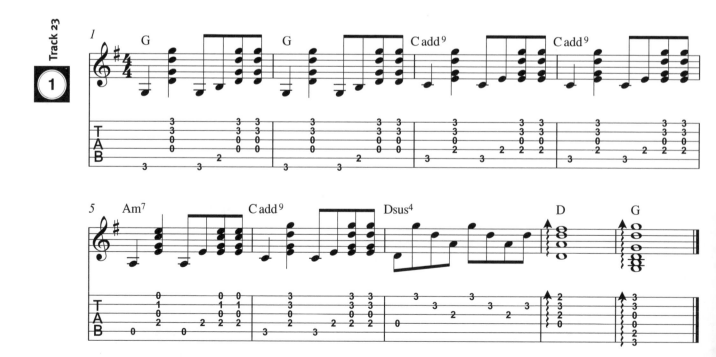

DAY 21

WEEK 3 TEST

Well, here we are again, and give yourself a pat on the back if you've been sticking

religiously to your routine. You've learned a lot of new chords this week, as well as

some vital terms and symbols that will enable you to read charts of your favourite

songs when you've finished this book. Now it's time for your weekly jam track, but

before I let you play it's time for your weekly test, so pens at the ready...

1 What's the formula of a minor chord?

2 What is added to a minor chord to make it a minor seventh?

3 What's the purpose of a tie?

4 What's the formula of an add9 chord?

5 What is a coda?

Electric Guitar

WEEK 3 STUDY PIECE

This week's study piece has a slightly more modern feel to it than our previous pieces and is based on the rhythmic style of Noel Gallagher. Oasis's material is great to learn when you're starting out, as it's all pretty straightforward to play and instantly recognisable for both you and your audience at home.

This piece uses all of the new techniques we've looked at – ties, broken chords with arpeggios, etc – plus all of our new chords. Try to get an authentic, slightly overdriven sound with a jangly tone for this track. Also, aim to make the rhythm flowing and open. Enjoy.

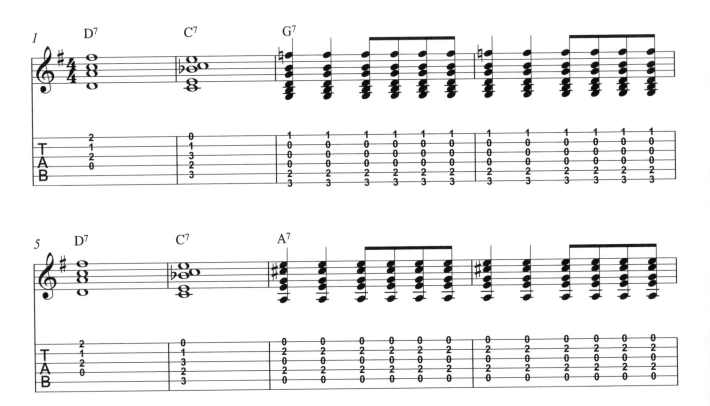

Electric Guitar

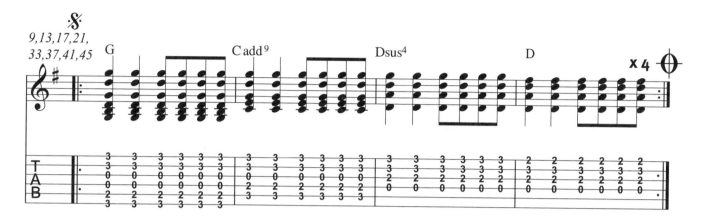

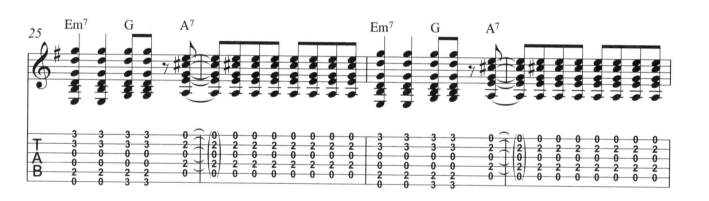

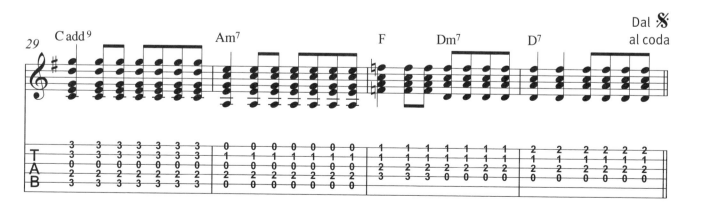

continues...

Electric Guitar

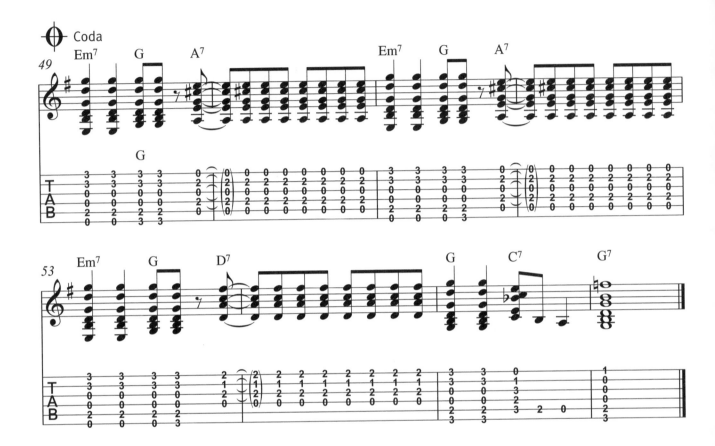

WEEK 4

OVERVIEW

We're now entering our fourth week, so I hope the finger soreness is starting to subside a little. By now you should be getting quite a repertoire of chords and study pieces under your belt. This week is going to be a little tough as we really start to push your chord knowledge. Here are the main goals for this week:

- To learn about movable chords;
- To look at the CAGED system;
- To look at progressions using the CAGED system.

Electric Guitar

DAY 22: THE CAGED SYSTEM

Today's lesson is designed to teach you an approach to playing chords and scales and is possibly the most important lesson you'll ever learn. One of the biggest problems when learning the guitar is finding ways to remember chord and scale shapes; they need to be organised in a way that will be easy to remember so they're there whenever you need them. When you're on stage, you can't just stand there thumbing frantically through a chord book.

QUOTE FOR THE WEEK

People don't consider me a guitar player because I'm the rhythm player, but rhythm is important and I love playing it.

– Ray Davis, The Kinks

First you need to learn your chords, and to do this we're going to use a system known as the *CAGED system*. This system uses the five basic major chord shapes of C, A, G, E and D. You've already learned the open positions of these chords, but now you need to learn how to make them into movable (ie barre) shapes.

As this approach takes quite a while to get your head around, the best way to learn it is by doing a few shapes at a time. To start with, we're going to learn how to change the chords of E and A into movable shapes. First we need to find the root notes of both shapes, as this is the note that allows us to move the shapes around. (Remember that the root note is the note that gives the chord its name.) Before you move these shapes, you'll need to change the fingering so that the first finger is left unused.

Exercise 1 shows the E-shape barre, with the root note (circled) located on the sixth string. Once you've refretted the E shape with the second, third and fourth fingers, shift the shape up one fret, but make sure you keep the distance between the notes the same:

Exercise 1

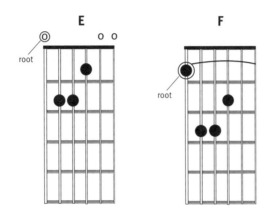

When you move the shape, you'll have to compensate for the open strings, and as the chord shape has been raised by one fret, you need to raise the open strings by one fret, too. To do this, take the partial barre you learned back on Day 19 and extend it across all six strings. Make sure that the pressure is even across the strings and that the notes you produce are clean and clear. When you've moved the chord, the root is still situated on the sixth string, but this time it's at the first fret and it's no longer E. Our E chord has been transformed into the chord of F major.

The picture over the page should give you an idea of how the shape should look:

Electric Guitar

Exercise 2 shows the A chord as a movable shape. Once again, the trick is to refinger the shape to be able to move it. First hold down the D, G and B strings with the third finger to form a partial barre, then shift the shape up by one fret. Remember that you'll have to shift the open strings by the same amount, so once you've shifted the shape – in effect, turning the A chord into a chord of A♯/B♭ – apply the barre at the first fret, raising the root note from the open A to A♯ (B♭). You'll notice that this chord has two names, and is thus known as an *enharmonic*.

Exercise 2

Track 26

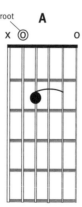

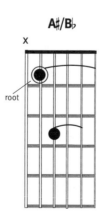

114

The picture below shows how to fret the A barre shape:

 It's vital to remember that the root note is the note that gives the chord its name. To move a chord around, simply move the whole thing so that the root note falls on the note that you want the chord to become. For instance, if you want to play the chord of A using an E shape, simply move the shape so that the root note falls on the fifth fret of the sixth string.

Electric Guitar

DAY 23: MORE CAGED SHAPES

Today you'll be learning more about CAGED shapes. Yesterday you learned how to change E and A chords into movable barre chord shapes, and today we'll be looking at how to shift C and D shapes. All of the same rules apply with these shapes: first you have to refinger the chords, keeping the first finger free, to enable you to apply the barre with it and then move the shapes about.

Exercise 1 shows how to turn the C shape into a movable barre chord. First, refinger the chords with the second, third and fourth fingers, keeping the first finger free. Once you've shifted the shape up by one fret, apply a partial bar across the top three strings. (The root note of the C shape is on the A string.) As you've shifted the shape one fret higher, the chord has changed to C#/D♭ major.

Exercise 1

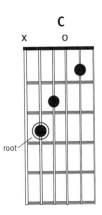

Exercise 2 shows you how to turn the D shape into a barre shape. Once again, follow the same procedure by refingering the chord with the second, third and fourth fingers, shift the shape up one fret and then apply the barre. This will raise the D chord to a D♯/E♭ major chord.

Exercise 2

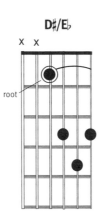

Electric Guitar

Exercise 3 is a short chord progression that swaps between the E and the A shapes to help you learn the positions of the root notes on the bottom E and A strings. First, before you can play this exercise, you need to learn the notes on the bottom two strings. Remember that the root of the E shape is on the E string and the root of the A shape is on the A string. Here is a list of the notes on frets 1–12 on the bottom E string:

F	F#/Gb	G	G#/Ab	A	A#/Bb	B	C	C#/Db	D	D#/Eb	E
1	2	3	4	5	6	7	8	9	10	11	12

Now here's a list of the notes found at frets 1–12 on the A string:

A#/Bb	B	C	C#/Db	D	D#/Eb	E	F	F#/Gb	G	G#/Ab	A
1	2	3	4	5	6	7	8	9	10	11	12

These two lists should help you to move the two barre chord shapes to the chords found in the chord progression shown in Exercise 3 – which, you'll notice, are played on adjacent frets. When you're playing them, say their names out loud so that they really sink in:

Exercise 3

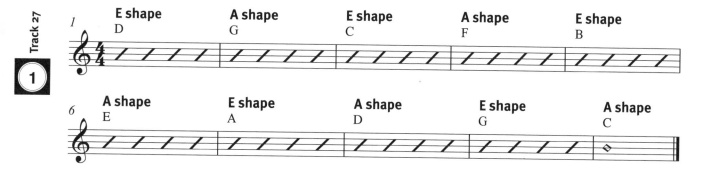

Exercise 4 is the reverse version of Exercise 3, starting with the A shape and moving to the E shape:

Exercise 4

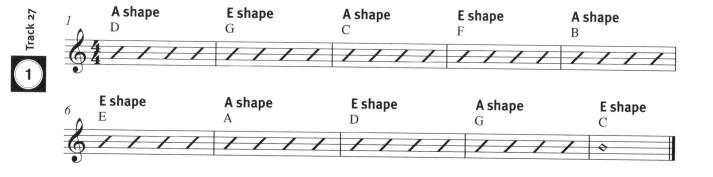

Electric Guitar

DAY 24: EVEN MORE CAGED SHAPES AND MOVABLE POWER CHORDS

Today you'll be learning the final shape of the CAGED system: the G shape. This is the trickiest of all the five shapes, as it involves a particularly wide stretch. Once again, the trick is to refinger the G shape using the second, third and fourth fingers, leaving the first finger free to apply as a barre.

Exercise 1 shows how to move the G shape around the neck. Once you've refingered the chord, move the shape up one fret, and then of course you'll have to compensate for the shift by fretting the strings that were open. This is where the stretch occurs, so make sure that all of the notes are clean and unmuted. As the root of the open G shape is located on the third fret of the bottom E string, when the chord is shifted the root moves to the fourth fret of the bottom E to produce the new chord of G♯/A♭ major.

Exercise 1

1

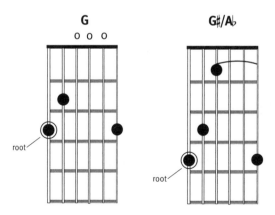

Exercise 2 shows a very important variation on the E shape: the movable E5 shape.

The root of this chord is on the sixth string, as it is with the full major shape, but

unlike the full shape, this one uses only three strings. Here the chord has its root

on the third fret of the sixth string, giving us a G5 power chord:

Exercise 2

G5

Track 28

①

Exercise 3 shows the A5 movable shape, which is the same shape as the movable

E5 but dropped onto the next set of strings. The root note lies at the third fret of

the A string, giving us a C5 power chord:

Electric Guitar

Exercise 3

C5

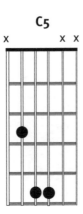

I've tried to keep some continuity with the chords we're moving here, so as we've been moving power chords I've also moved our sixth and dominant seventh variations that we used for our blues riffs.

Exercises 4 and 5 include the movable versions of the E6 and E7 shapes. These shapes take a little practise to perfect because, as you can see, the stretches are pretty wide:

Exercise 4

G6

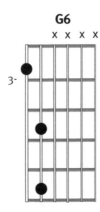

Exercise 5

Track 28

Exercises 6 and 7 illustrate C versions of the movable A6 and A7 shape. As you can see, these shapes are the same as the E-shape version, just dropped down onto the A string:

Exercise 6

Track 28

Exercise 7

Track 28

Exercise 8 is our last exercise of the day and makes use of the C and D shapes. You've already learned the notes on the E and A strings, and as the C shape has its root on

Electric Guitar

the A string, you can move the shape around. But we'll need to have a look at the notes found on the D string before you can move the D shape around. Here they are:

D♯/E♭	E	F	F♯/G♭	G	G♯/A♭	A	A♯/B♭	B	C	C♯/D♭	D
1	2	3	4	5	6	7	8	9	10	11	12

Now you should be able to move the D shape around and locate all of the chords in the progression. As a little extra exercise, try moving the G shape around. (Remember that the root of this chord is on the sixth string.)

Exercise 8

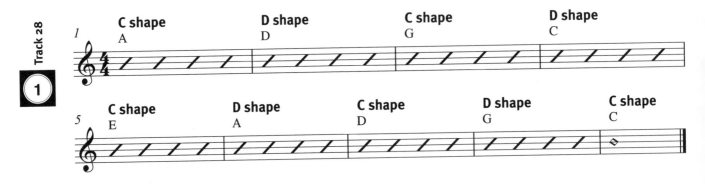

DAY 25: FIVE CHORDS PER KEY

So far you've been moving each of the CAGED shapes around and locating the root notes. You've also been getting used to being able to play the new shapes and handle the wider stretches.

Now we're really going to see the benefits of learning the CAGED system. Today we're going to concentrate on using all five shapes to play one key. This will enable you to play any chord in any position and allow you to change chords by doing more than moving just one or two shapes around, and it will also make your writing sound more melodic. Often it sounds much better to change to a chord that's in close proximity, by using another shape, than jumping to a different position using the same movable shape. This technique of playing five shapes per key will also help with your general knowledge of the fingerboard, as later you'll be learning scales based on these shapes.

First you need to be aware of how the CAGED shapes link together. Basically, they all connect in the order of the letters in the word CAGED.

If we start on the C shape, the root on the A string links us to the A shape. The D, G and B strings played in the A shape link us to the G shape, and the root note of this shape is on the E string, which is shared by the E shape. This shape has its root on the D string, which links us to the root of the D shape, and then the top three strings of the D shape link us back to the C shape. So you can see that all of the shapes link together; no matter what shape you start on, the next shape will be the next letter of the word CAGED.

Electric Guitar

Exercise 1 shows all five positions of the A chord using the five CAGED shapes. It starts off with the open position A shape, which is then linked to the G shape, with its root on the fifth fret of the bottom E string. The next shape is the E shape, the root of which is on the same string, and this is then linked to the D shape, which shares the note located at the seventh fret of the D string. The top three strings of the D shape then link back to the C shape. All of the shapes are the chord of A, which means that you can cover the entire neck with one chord!

Exercise 1

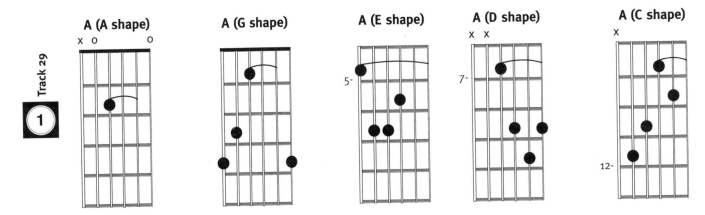

Exercise 2 uses the same procedure as the previous example, but this time you're going to learn the five shapes of the B major chord. As you now know how this approach works, I've just listed the order of the shapes: A, G, E, D and C.

Electric Guitar

Exercise 2

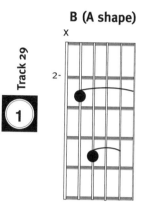

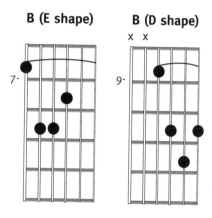

Exercise 3 is the final example of the day. In this example you're going to learn all five positions of the C major chord. Here the shapes are in the order C, A, G, E and D.

Exercise 3

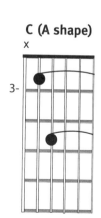

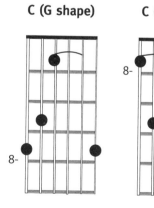

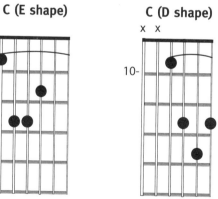

Electric Guitar

DAY 26: MORE CAGED CHORDS

Today we're going to look at more keys in five fingerboard positions. As your chord vocabulary is beginning to grow, it's important that you make a note of the keys you've learned. When practising new keys, it's always a good idea to say the root-note position out loud so that it really sinks in.

Exercise 1 includes all five positions of the D major chord, with its shapes listed in the order D, C, A, G and E. Make sure you remember the position of the root notes of each shape:

Exercise 1

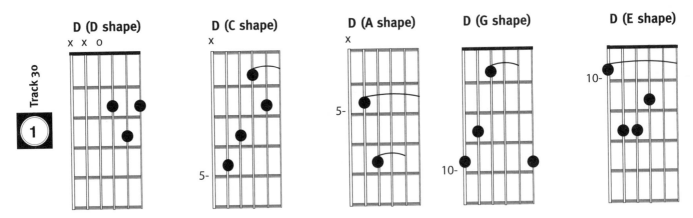

Exercise 2 shows all five positions of the E chord using the CAGED shapes, shown in the order E, D, C, A and G:

Electric Guitar

Exercise 2

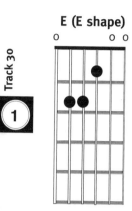

E (E shape)

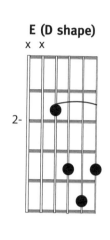

E (D shape)

E (C shape)

E (A shape)

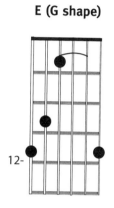

E (G shape)

Exercise 3 includes all five positions of the F major chord, shown in the order E, D, C, A and G:

Exercise 3

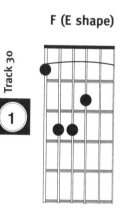

F (E shape)

F (D shape)

F (C shape)

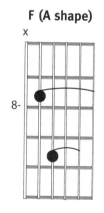

F (A shape)

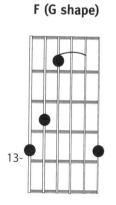

F (G shape)

Exercise 4 is today's final example and covers all of the shapes of the G major chord, listing them in the order G, E, D, C and A:

Electric Guitar

Exercise 4

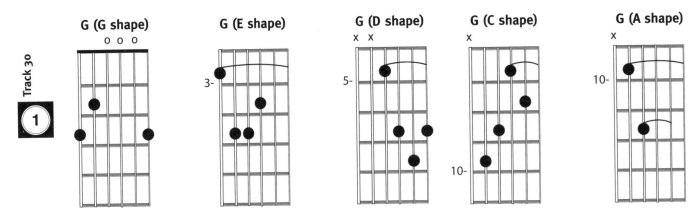

You should now have a fairly large knowledge of major chords – and this list includes only the natural chords; there are 12 keys in total, with five shapes per chord, giving us a grand total of 60 chords. Who says you need a chord book?

DAY 27: PUTTING THE SHAPES INTO PRACTICE

Today I've set you only one assignment, but this will probably serve you well in your practice for many years to come. Now that you've got all these chords at your disposal, it's time to put them into use, so I've come up with a pretty straightforward progression. The idea is that you perform it using all five shapes from the CAGED system.

There are two ways in which you should practise the progression shown here. The first is to play it in five separate positions, each based on the five CAGED shapes, the idea being that you change between chords using the nearest possible shape. Start each time with C, as played it as a C, A, G, E or D shape, and then change to the nearest possible shape for the other chords.

The other idea is to jump randomly to any shape. Working this way will help you to develop a good knowledge of root notes on the neck, and it will also work your left-hand accuracy. Have fun!

Exercise 1

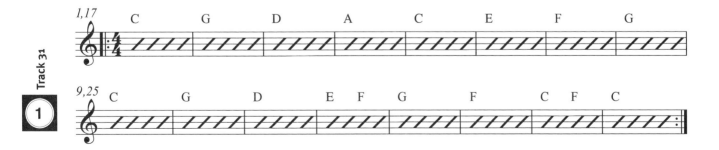

Electric Guitar

DAY 28

WEEK 4 TEST

Here we are again, and wow! What a full-on week. Who would've thought you'd know this many chords this early on? Anyway, before the Week 4 jam track, its time for a short test.

---

1   What is the CAGED system?

2   Which two shapes have their roots on the E string?

3   Which two shapes have their roots on the A string?

4   What's the total number of major chords available in every key using the CAGED system?

5   What word describes a chord that's called by two different names – ie G♯/A♭?

Electric Guitar

WEEK 4 STUDY PIECE

Today's fun-packed study piece uses a mixture of movable power chords and major chords, and is reminiscent of the style of bands such as The Kinks and The Black Crowes. It also includes a few flat chords – namely E♭ and B♭ – so check the fret positions of these carefully. Also look out for the stretch with the movable sixth chords. Try to copy the tone quality on the CD to give a slight retro crunch.

continues...

133

Electric Guitar

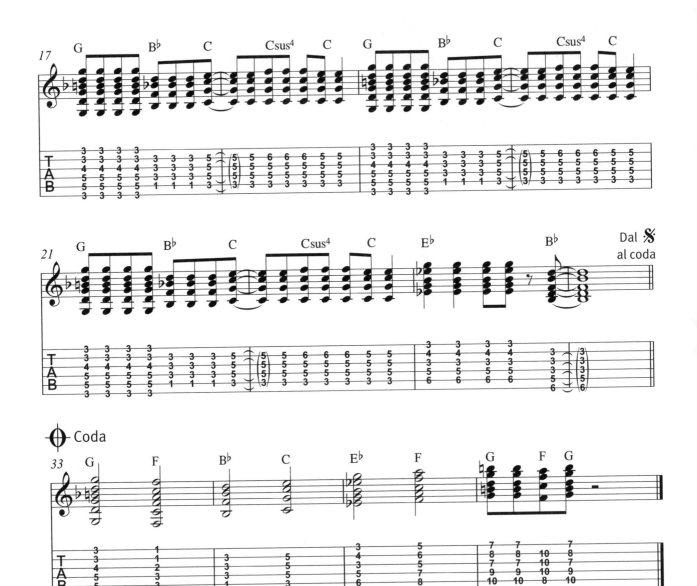

WEEK 5

OVERVIEW

Here we are at the beginning of another week, and what a week it's going to be! There's a lot of ground to cover this week, and the intensity of the lessons is starting to kick up a gear, so grab your guitar and a cup of coffee. Here's what we'll be covering this week:

- CAGED major scales;
- Movable minor chords;
- Scale sequences;
- The cycle of fourths;
- New rhythms.

Electric Guitar

DAY 29: THE CAGED MAJOR SCALE

Your main task of the week is to begin to understand the major scale system. Many guitarists shy away from the major scale to start with. In fact, I did this myself, as the only exposure I'd had to the scale was in pretty lame school music lessons. I just couldn't see how it would aid me in my journey as a rock guitarist. But the reality is that the major scale forms the basis of pretty much all Western music. The more I explored my favourite

QUOTE FOR THE WEEK

I don't think about what I do – I really don't. Put it this way: you've only got 12 notes, and how you use them is up to you.

– Edward Van Halen

players, the more I discovered just how many ways the scale is used. Eventually I used

the scale to understand modes, and it's now an integral part of my playing.

There are two main ways of learning the major scale: via three-note-per-string patterns (which we'll look at later) and via CAGED scales, based on the CAGED chord shapes. The latter system is an excellent way of remembering the scales, as you can simply relate them to the chord shapes. Eventually, you'll find this very beneficial when soloing over chord changes, and also for sight-reading.

The major scale is a scale comprising seven notes (OK, eight if you include the octave of the root) and is made up from a formula, or template, which is universal in all major keys. Once you've learned the system in one key, it will transpose very easily to the remaining keys.

The formula is as follows:

Tone → Tone → Semitone → Tone → Tone → Tone → Semitone

In the key of C major, for instance, the scale is as follows:

C   D   E   F   G   A   B   C

 Although all of the notes of the major scale are very important and should be learned, for now you just need to spend some time learning the position of the root note, as this will allow you to move the scale easily into all of the 11 other keys and to find them around specific chord shapes.

Exercise 1 shows the C shape of the C major chord, and on the right is the scale shape based on it. Make sure that you pay attention to the root notes:

Exercise 1

C (C shape)

Exercise 2 shows the C major chord based on the A chord shape. Next to it is the C major scale based on the A chord shape. Once again, be sure to pay attention to the root notes:

Exercise 2

C (A shape)

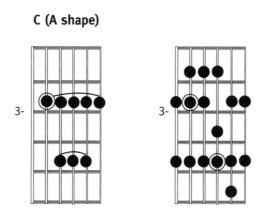

If you look closely, you'll notice that both scale shapes share the same root note, and that they actually dovetail together.

Exercise 3 features a sequence that starts on the lowest root note and includes all the notes in that position on the neck in the key of C major. The exercise resolves with the chord of C in its native C shape:

Electric Guitar

Exercise 3

Exercise 4 features a run that starts on the lowest root note in the key of C and includes all the notes in the same position. It resolves with the chord of C, but in the movable A shape.

Exercise 4

Electric Guitar

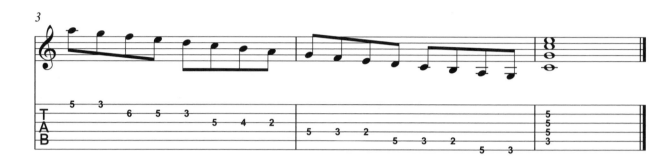

Electric Guitar

DAY 30: MORE SCALES!

Today we're going to learn two more CAGED scale shapes and put them into a practical exercise. When you've learnt these, make sure you combine them with yesterday's scales. Exercise 1 includes the scale of C major based on the G shape of the C major chord:

Exercise 1

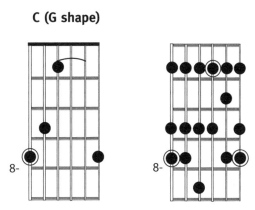

The C scale in Exercise 2 is based on the CAGED chord shape of E major. Make sure you remember the roots of both shapes:

Exercise 2

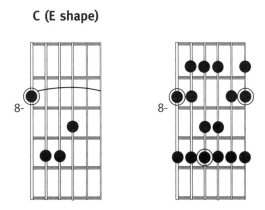

Electric Guitar

Exercise 3 includes a scale sequence that starts on the root and includes all the notes of the C major scale in that position on the neck. The exercise resolves with the movable G shape of the C major chord:

Exercise 3

Exercise 4 is today's final exercise and includes the C major based on the movable E shape. The passage starts on the root and eventually resolves to the C major chord:

Electric Guitar

Exercise 4

Electric Guitar

DAY 31: SCALE SEQUENCES

Today we're going to look at our final CAGED scale shape, and then we'll look at

ways of practising them in the form of scale exercises. Not only are these exercises

good for learning the shapes, but they're also excellent for developing technique.

Exercise 1 includes our final shape and includes a C major scale based on the D

movable shape. Don't forget to memorise the root notes:

Exercise 1

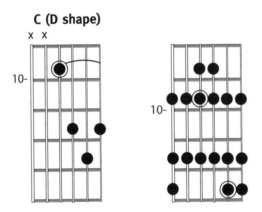

Exercise 2 includes a passage based on a C major scale that starts on the lowest

possible root and includes all the notes in that position. The passage resolves with

the relevant movable shape: C major as a movable D major shape:

Exercise 2

Exercise 3 uses alternate picking and ascends in groups of four, starting on each note in turn:

Exercise 3

continues...

Electric Guitar

Exercise 3 continued

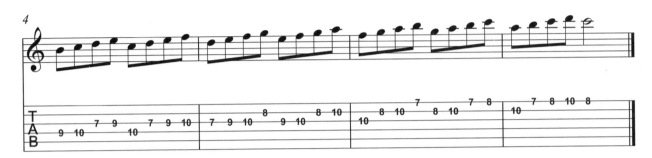

Exercise 4 is the descending version of the previous exercise:

Exercise 4

When you have the sequence of the exercise under your fingers, make sure you

duplicate it through the remaining scale shapes.

Exercise 5 shows a neck diagram that illustrates all of the patterns combined. It's easy to see how learning these shapes will enable you to memorise the entire neck, which really frees you up when you start improvising.

Exercise 5

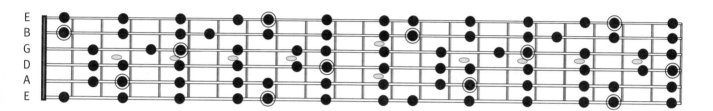

C major scale – all positions
⬤ = C note

Electric Guitar

DAY 32: NEW RHYTHMS, CHORDS AND SCALE EXERCISES

Today we have something of a mixed bag to get through. To start with, there are some new rhythmic patterns to practise, plus some new chords, but there are also some more scale exercises to get through. You didn't think I'd let you off that easily, did you?

So far you've learned quite a few rhythmic patterns for playing chord parts. Today we're going to revisit the triplet and look at some combination patterns.

Exercise 1 includes a triplet strumming pattern. Although I explained about triplets in Week 2, it's a good idea to revisit them here and just make sure you can remember how to play them.

Exercise 1

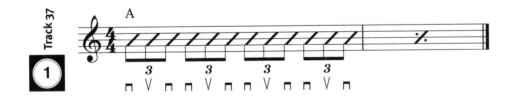

Exercise 2 includes a straight 16th-note rhythmic pattern. Again, this is just to refresh your memory, as you've been playing a few scales recently.

Exercise 2

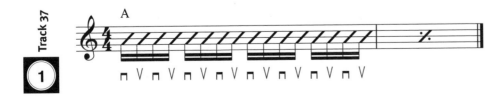

Exercise 3 includes a four-bar sequence that features four separate 16th-note patterns, all of which mix both quarter-note and eighth-note rhythms. These variations are very useful and are common patterns.

Exercise 3

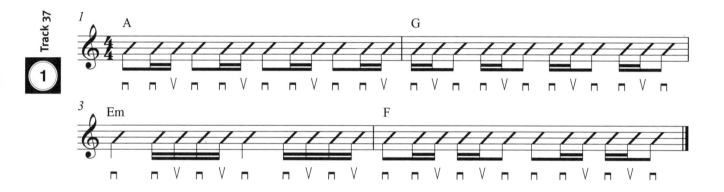

Exercise 4 includes a movable E minor chord shape. This moves in the same way as the major version to produce any other minor chord, such as the F minor shown here:

Exercise 4

Electric Guitar

Exercise 5 includes the movable A minor shape, which also works in the same way as the movable major version. When you move the A minor shape up two frets, for instance, you get a chord of B minor. This shape can be played at all frets, giving 12 more minor chords, and a total so far of 24. See where this is going?

Exercise 5

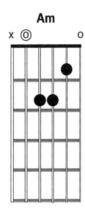
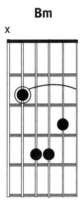

Exercise 6 includes a new scale exercise, an ascending sequence that uses alternate picking and an eighth-note triplet rhythm:

Exercise 6

Exercise 6 continued

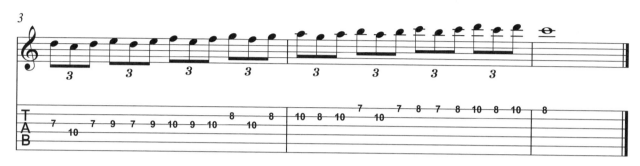

Exercise 7 is the descending version of the previous exercise:

Exercise 7

Track 37

Electric Guitar

DAY 33: RESTS AND THE CYCLE OF FOURTHS

Today you'll be learning how to use eighth-note and 16th-note rests. You'll also be practising the major scale in all 12 keys, with a little help from a key cycle.

Exercise 1 includes our first rest, the eighth-note rest, which appears on the downbeat to give a reggae-style rhythm.

Exercise 1

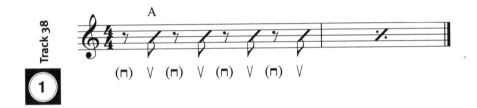

Exercise 2 includes the same rest, but now the eighth notes have been replaced with pairs of 16th notes:

Exercise 2

Exercises 3–6 all include variations of this idea and also include some 16th-note rests (𝄿). This type of rhythm playing is very important; funk and reggae styles in particular rely heavily on syncopation, where the accent is on the upbeat and the downbeat is rested.

Exercise 3

Exercise 4

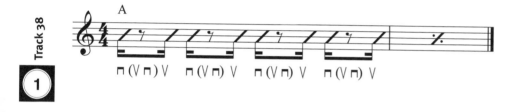

Exercise 5

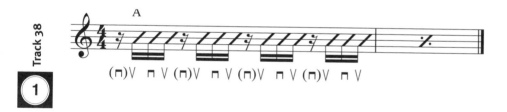

Exercise 6

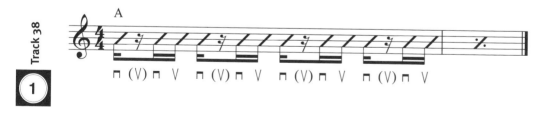

Now I'm going to talk a little about theory. Hopefully some of you have tried to play your CAGED major scale shapes in others keys. If you want to learn them in an effective and efficient manner, it's pointless just shifting randomly around the

Electric Guitar

neck, as this is a disorganised way to practise and it won't help you to remember

your scales.

The most effective way of remembering the scales is by practising them in a melodic

sequence through all 12 keys. The way I do this is by employing a technique known

as the *cycle of fourths*. The basic idea is that you shift from one scale to another

that's four notes apart (ie an interval of a perfect fourth). If you carry on in this vein,

you'll pass through all of the 12 keys and end up back where you started, completing

a cycle. Here are all of the keys in the order they appear in the cycle of fourths:

The Cycle Of Fourths

C F Bb Eb Ab Db Gb/F# B E A D G C

You'll notice that when you reach the halfway mark, Gb, the note is also shown as its

enharmonic equivalent, F#. This is because up to that point all of the keys contained

flats, but from B onwards they all contain sharps. (C major, of course, contains no

sharp or flats – all the notes are *natural*.) Armed with this tool, you can now play

through all of the keys using the five CAGED shape, giving you a total of 60 scales!

Exercise 7 includes our first cycle of fourths sequence. With this exercise, you'll be

running through all of the keys, changing to the nearest possible shape each time.

This means that, when you play over chord changes, you'll be able to change key

seamlessly, as all of the scales are under your fingertips. The scales have been

condensed to single octave patterns to give you an even scale in each bar.

154

Electric Guitar

Exercise 7

Electric Guitar

DAY 34: NEW CHORDS AND MORE KEY CYCLES

I've split today's lessons into two sections, one containing some hip new chords and the other is a continuation of the cycle of fourths. Today we'll look at the next positions for all of the scales.

Exercise 1 includes some more suspended chords: Asus2, Asus4, Esus4, Csus4 and Csus2. These work great when played as a variation on major chords:

Exercise 1

Track 39

1

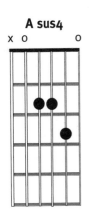 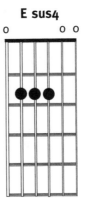 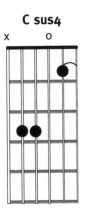 

Exercise 2 includes our next major scale position in the cycle of fourths. Once again, these are ascending one octave patterns. When you have them under your fingers, try playing continuously through both positions – this one and the one we looked at earlier. You can also extend them to the full shape. These scale exercises are pretty tough though and should be practised and learned over a period of time.

Electric Guitar

Exercise 2

Electric Guitar

DAY 35

WEEK 5 TEST

Here we are again, and what a lot we got through this week! Obviously, I'm trying to cram in as much as possible, so remember that some of the studies should be continued after you've completed this book and will form the basis for more advanced playing and practice. Now let's see how you're getting on so far.

1   What's the formula for the major scale?

2   Name the notes of the C major scale.

3   What is the cycle of fourths?

4   Write out the cycle of fourths.

5   What is syncopation?

Electric Guitar

WEEK 5 STUDY PIECE

Here's your end-of-week jam track, which includes yet another different style: reggae. The syncopated rhythms featured here will help you no end with your rhythm playing, so keep it tight. I've included quite a few of the new barre chords covered this week, plus a couple of scale runs, just so you get used to using them. Have fun!

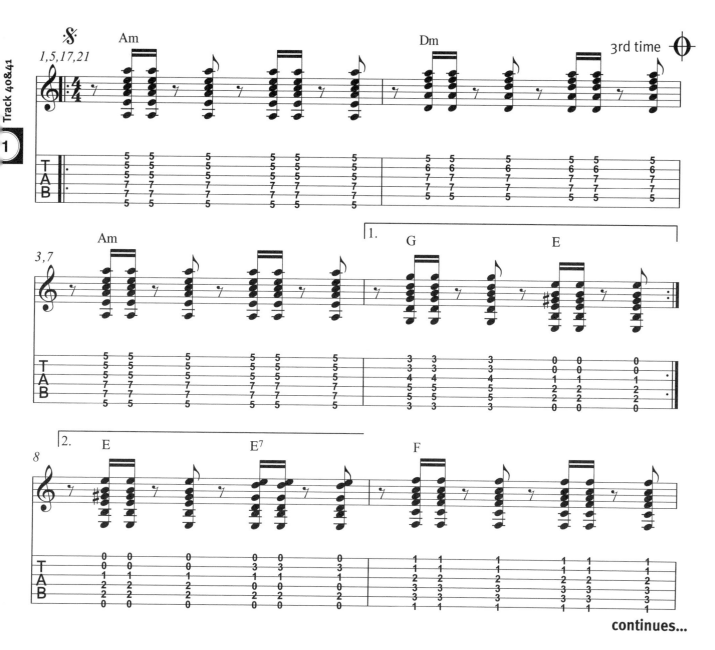

continues...

Electric Guitar

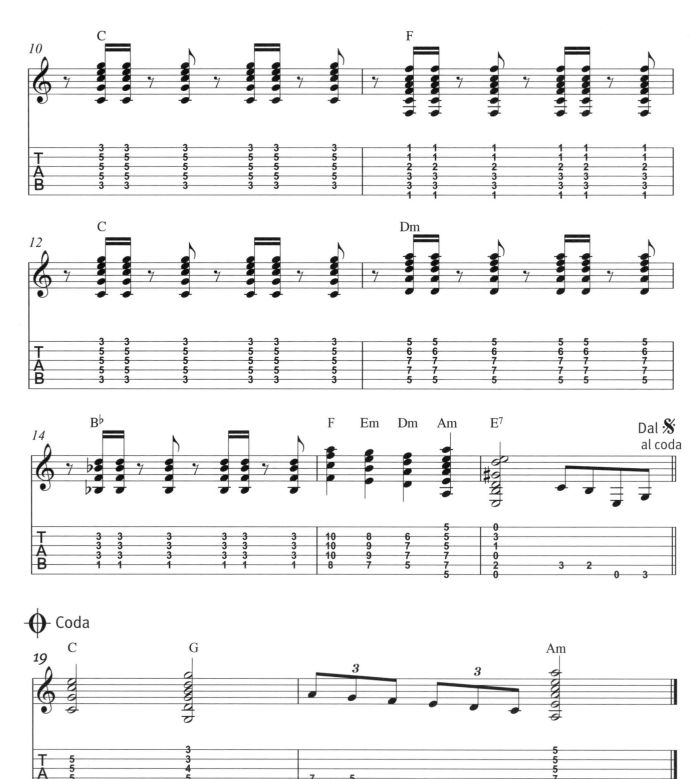

WEEK 6

OVERVIEW

Here we are at week 6, and by now you should have a good stockpile of chords and scales, and with the scale exercises covered last week your technique should be coming together nicely. This week's lessons contain yet more information to absorb about chords and scales, and provides an introduction to the realm of harmony.

Here's a breakdown of what we'll be doing this week:

- Finishing our cycle of fourths studies;
- Completing our minor CAGED chords;
- Learning the harmonised major scale;
- Learning the Nashville numbering system;
- Learning some new chords and extensions.

Electric Guitar

DAY 36: MORED CAGED SCALE PRACTICE AND NEW MINOR CHORDS

Today we're going to continue with our major scale cycle of fourths sequence, completing the next position of the fingerboard. You'll also be improving your chord knowledge by looking at the final three shapes of the CAGED minor chords.

So far you've learned how to turn the chords of E minor and A minor into movable shapes. As we did with the major shapes, we're now going to include the other three shapes to complete the CAGED minor shapes. I know I've already mentioned this, but it's worth saying again: The difference between a major and a minor chord is only one note. We simply take the major third of the chord and lower it by one semitone to produce a minor third.

Exercise 1 shows you how to play a D minor chord. To turn it into a movable shape, simply refinger the chord, keeping the first finger free, then shift the chord up one fret and apply the barre at the first fret. The root note of D minor is situated on the D string, and it still is when you move your fingers up the frets.

All you have to do to turn the chord into any minor chord is simply shift it until the root of the chord lands on the note of the chord you wish to play. The example in Exercise 1 shows the chord shifted up two frets, with the root note now situated on the second fret of the D string to give the chord of E minor.

Electric Guitar

Exercise 1

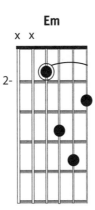

Exercise 2 introduces the C minor chord shape. This chord is quite tricky to hold, and as it contains a flattened third – ie E♭ – make sure you don't strike the open top E string or it will sound very wrong. The movable version of the shape is a little awkward, but it will get your fingers stretching. Here I've shifted it by two frets, so that the root is on the fifth fret of the A string, resulting in a D minor chord:

Exercise 2

Electric Guitar

Exercise 3 is our final look at movable minor chords and is based on the G minor shape. The open position involves a partial bar across the top three strings, while the movable appears here in two versions: the first involving the partial barre (which is a bit of a stretch) and the second featuring a slightly easier voicing. Here the chord has been moved up two frets, with the root now on the E string, fifth fret, to produce a chord of A minor:

Exercise 3

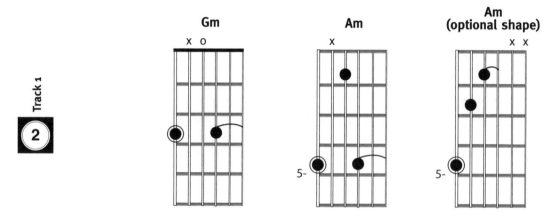

Exercise 4 carries on from last week and includes another position of the CAGED scale sequence. Once again, these one octave patterns are shown ascending only. By now you should be able to cover quite a lot of the neck with all the scales we've looked at – in all 12 keys!

Exercise 4

Electric Guitar

DAY 37: MINOR CHORD PROGRESSIONS AND MORE SCALES

Today we're going to look at a progression that includes a mixture of both major and minor chords and makes a great workout for our CAGED patterns. I've also included yet another position of the scale exercise we looked at earlier.

DAY 37 STUDY PIECES

Exercise 1 includes a short study piece to get you into the swing of things. This progression uses a mixture of major and minor chords, and although I've only shown it played through once, you can just keep on repeating it.

There are two ways for you to practise this sequence. The first involves keeping the chords in one position of the neck, combining many of the CAGED chord shapes, and the second is to move around the neck as much as you can. The second approach will help you to recognise root notes quickly and efficiently so that you never find yourself stuck for a chord. For future studies, try writing out your own progressions and using a mixture of chords.

Exercise 1

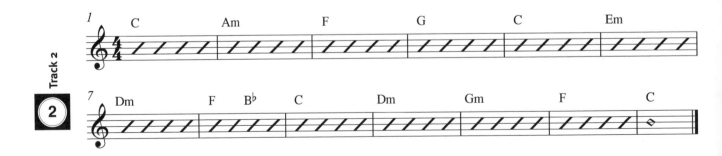

Electric Guitar

Exercise 2 includes the next position of our scale study, played through all 12 keys in a cycle of fourths. Just one more position to go and you'll know all of the major scales, all over the neck!

Exercise 2

continues...

Electric Guitar

Exercise 2 continued

Electric Guitar

DAY 38: THE MINOR SCALE

Today we're going to look at a minor scale based on the minor CAGED chords. We'll also complete our major scale study and look at some new time signatures. Some of you may be feeling the strain of all of these scales, but hang in there. Remember, they'll serve you well long after you've completed this Crash Course, so try to make them part of your daily practice routine.

Before we look at the minor scale, you first need to study some theory. Just like the major, the minor scale has a formula governing the distance (ie intervals) between the notes – for instance, here's the interval list and notes of the C major scale:

C Major Scale

```
C   D   E   F   G   A   B   C
1   2   3   4   5   6   7   1
```

The formula for the minor scale is simply a variation of the major scale formula and is as follows: 1, 2, ♭3, 4, 5, ♭6, ♭7, 1. If we take this formula and adopt A as the root note, we get the following scale:

A Minor Scale

```
A   B   C    D   E   F    G    A
1   2   ♭3   4   5   ♭6   ♭7   1
```

Electric Guitar

If you compare the notes of the C major and A minor scales, you'll see that they're the same; they simply start from a different root note. This means that these two scales are what's known as *relative* – C major is the relative major of A minor, and A minor is the relative minor of C major. This also means you can simply recycle the CAGED major scale shapes you learned in the key of C and start them from the A note to give you a whole bunch of A minor scales. This way of reapplying information is a great way of building up chord/scale knowledge without bogging you down with irrelevant shapes; so far all our shapes have been based on five variations.

Exercise 1 shows an A minor chord and the A minor scale shape. You should hopefully recognise this as the C shape of C major, except that it starts on the A note.

Exercise 1

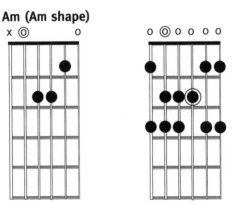

Exercise 2 shows the A minor chord based on the G minor shape. The scale shape on the right is the same shape as the C major scale shape based on the A-shape chord. Again, all we're doing is starting on the A to make it sound like A minor.

Electric Guitar

Exercise 2

Am (Gm shape)

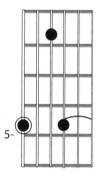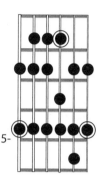

Exercise 3 is the A minor chord based on the E minor barre shape. The scale shape is the same as the C major based on the G shape, but once again it starts on A to produce a minor tonality.

Exercise 3

Am (Em shape)

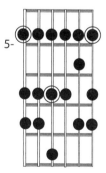

Exercise 4 is there for you if you feel that you haven't learnt enough scales for one day! You'll be pleased to know that this is the final cycle of fourths exercise, using

Electric Guitar

all 12 major scales. If you've got this far, you can now play every major scale in every position. Congratulations!

Exercise 4

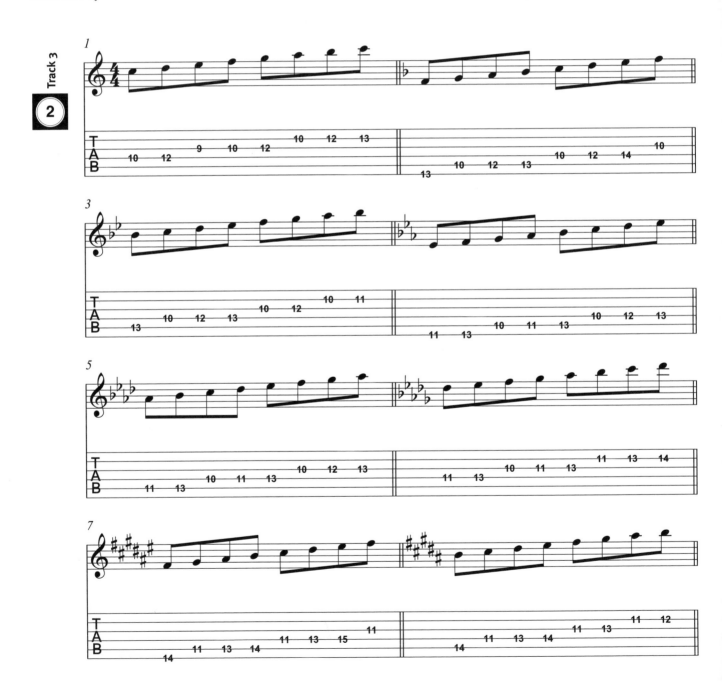

Electric Guitar

Exercise 4 continued

Just to round things off today, let's take a look at some new time signatures. As I said earlier, in a time signature the top number tells you how many beats are in each a bar while the bottom number indicates how long each beat is. A 4 represents a quarter note, a 2 represents a half note and an 8 represents an eighth note.

Exercise 5 includes some rhythms in 3/4, which means that there are three quarter notes to a bar. This time signature gives the feeling of a waltz.

Exercise 5

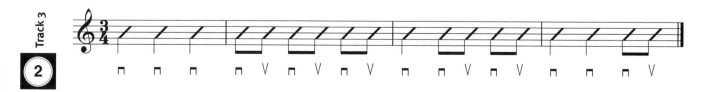

173

Electric Guitar

Exercise 6 includes some rhythms in 6/8 time, which means that there are sixth eighth notes to a bar, grouped in threes:

Exercise 6

Exercise 7 is today's final example and shows some rhythms in 12/8 time, which means that there are twelve eighth notes to a bar, again grouped in threes. This type of rhythm is common in blues, giving a swing triplet feel.

Exercise 7

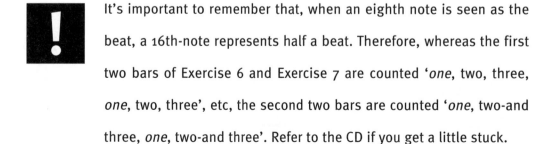

It's important to remember that, when an eighth note is seen as the beat, a 16th-note represents half a beat. Therefore, whereas the first two bars of Exercise 6 and Exercise 7 are counted 'one, two, three, one, two, three', etc, the second two bars are counted 'one, two-and three, one, two-and three'. Refer to the CD if you get a little stuck.

DAY 39: MORE MINOR SCALES

Today we'll finish off our study of the minor scale system by having a look at the final two CAGED shapes. We'll also be looking at some practice sequences to help you memorise the scales and be able to associate them with the specific chord shapes.

Exercise 1 shows an A minor chord using the movable D minor chord shape. The A minor scale shape is also shown, based on the E shape of the C major scale but starting on A to produce an A minor sound.

Exercise 1

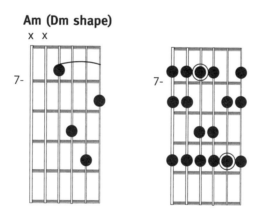

Exercise 2 shows an A minor chord based on the C minor chord shape. The scale shape shown with this chord is the D shape of the C major scale, except it uses A as its root note.

Electric Guitar

Exercise 2

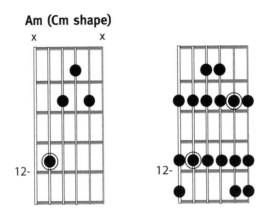

Am (Cm shape)

Now it's time for us to take a look at some minor scale practice sequences. To help you to memorise the scales here, all of the exercises start from the root and resolve on the root. Exercise 3 demonstrates the first scale shape, based on the A minor shape:

Exercise 3

Electric Guitar

Exercise 4 shows the next minor-scale shape, based on the G shape of the A minor chord:

Exercise 4

Exercise 5 shows the A minor scale based on the E minor movable chord shape:

Exercise 5

Exercise 6 shows the A minor scale based on the D minor movable chord shape:

Exercise 6

continues...

Electric Guitar

Exercise 6 continued

Exercise 7 is our final A minor scale shape and is based on the movable C minor

chord shape:

Exercise 7

178

 Now you've got the minor scale under your belt, try practising it in every key, using the cycle of fourths like you did with the major scale exercise we covered earlier. Although this exercise isn't shown here, it's important that you show initiative and start thinking things through for yourself. Try to find ways to expand musically.

Electric Guitar

DAY 40: THE HARMONISED MAJOR SCALE

Today you're going to learn a very important lesson in music theory: how to construct seven chords from the major scale. This idea will not only improve your knowledge base and allow you to come up with your own progressions, but it will also help you understand how to approach other progressions for soloing purposes. Later, it will also help you to understand modes.

First let's recap on some chord theory. There are three types of chord you need to understand: major, minor and diminished. The major chord adopts the formula 1–3–5, the minor chord uses the notes 1–♭3–5 and the diminished chord includes the notes 1–♭3–♭5.

The harmonised major scale is basically nothing more than a series of chords constructed from the major scale. The way it works is that each degree of the scale is a potential root note of a chord. Here's the order of chords found in the major scale:

Degree	Tonality
I	Major
ii	Minor
iii	Minor
IV	Major
V	Major
vi	Minor
vii	Diminished

If we use the scale of C major, we get the following set of chords:

Degree	Tonality
I	C major
ii	D minor
iii	E minor
IV	F major
V	G major
vi	A minor
vii	B diminished

This idea is universal for all keys and, if applied to other major scales, will give you a set of seven chords diatonic to any chosen key. Here are a few examples to get you started. Simply take each degree of the scale and treat it as the root of the chord, built from that scale step. Here, for example, are the diatonic chords of G major:

Degree	Tonality
I	G major
ii	A minor
iii	B minor
IV	C major
V	D major
vi	E minor
vii	F♯ diminished

Electric Guitar

Here are the chords of the A major scale:

Degree	Tonality
I	A major
ii	B minor
iii	C♯ minor
IV	D major
V	E major
vi	F♯ minor
vii	G♯ diminished

And finally here are the chords constructed from the D major scale:

Degree	Tonality
I	D major
ii	E minor
iii	F♯ minor
IV	G major
V	A major
vi	B minor
vii	C♯ diminished

From the examples shown here, you can see how easy it is to work out the chords of other keys as you encounter them.

You'll notice that the chords are labelled with Roman numerals. This idea enables you to write progressions down simply as numerals and then play them in whatever key you want. This technique is also referred to as the *Nashville number system*, as many Nashville session players would write out charts in this manner, so if the song was played by another artist who sang in a different key, they would have one universal chart. This idea of moving to other keys is known as *transposing*.

A typical progression from the major scale is the I–IV–V progression. In the key of C major, this would be C to F to G major. However, we could transpose this progression into another key simply by using the Nashville system. I–IV–V in G major would be G to C to D major or, in the key of A major, A to D to E major.

Before we look at the harmonised scale or any new exercises, you need to learn a new chord: the diminished chord. Exercise 1 includes several variations of the B diminished chord. The chords listed are based on the CAGED system, but I've included six shapes, as one is optional:

Exercise 1

Track 5

②

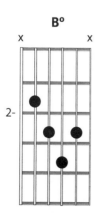

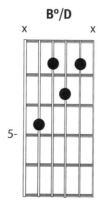

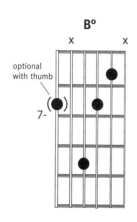

continues...

Electric Guitar

Exercise 1 continued

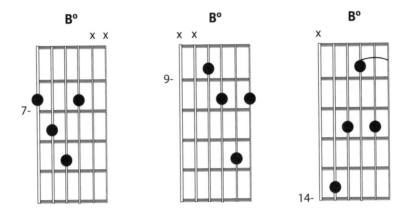

Exercise 2 includes the chords of the C major harmonised sale. All are played in the

open position and have been labelled with the relevant Roman numeral.

Exercise 2

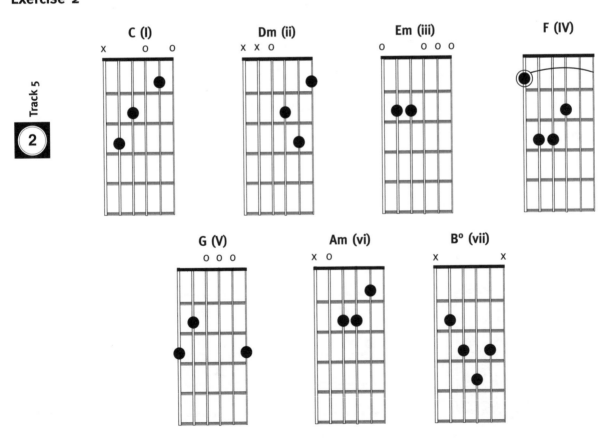

Electric Guitar

Exercise 3 includes the C harmonised major scale, but this time I've used some of the CAGED shapes. You could actually find five positions in which to play these seven chords, all based on the CAGED system:

Exercise 3

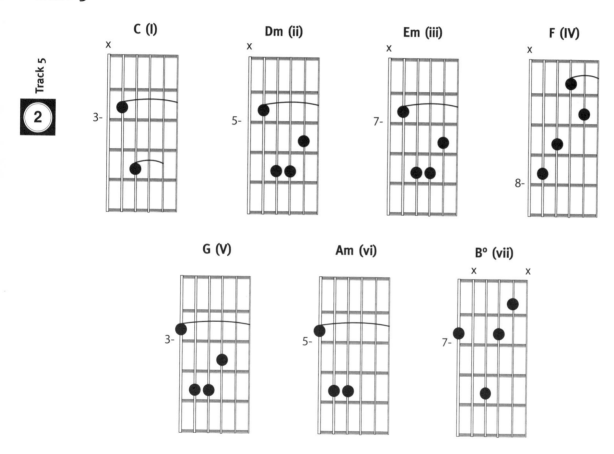

Exercises 4–6 are our final examples of the day. Here I've presented you with three short studies, but no chords have been written, only Roman numerals. Try playing these sequences in as many keys as you can. Start off by using the keys we've covered in this lesson.

Electric Guitar

Exercise 4

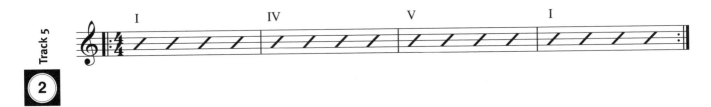

Exercise 5

Exercise 6

DAY 41: EXTENDED CHORDS

Today we're going to look at some common chord extensions and how to construct them around the CAGED system. We'll then look at their roles in the major scale.

Exercise 1 includes all five shapes of the C major seventh chord. As its name suggests, this is just a C major chord with the major seventh of the scale added to produce the formula 1, 3, 5, 7. This chord is very common in jazz.

Exercise 1

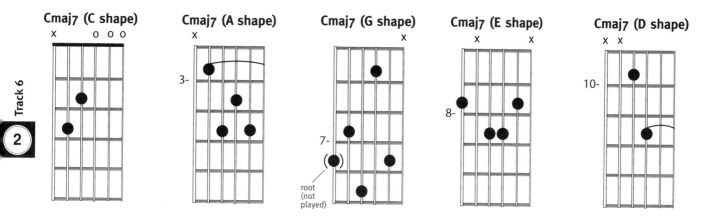

Exercise 2 includes all five CAGED shapes of the C minor seventh chord, which takes the formula 1, ♭3, 5, ♭7. This is a very useful chord extension and is found in many types of music.

Electric Guitar

Exercise 2

Track 6

2

Cm7 (C shape)	Cm7 (A shape)	Cm7 (G shape)	Cm7 (E shape)	Cm7 (D shape)

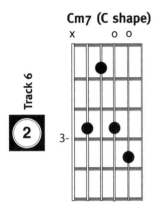 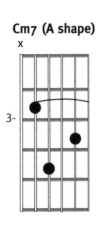 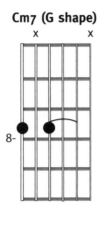 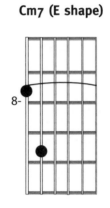 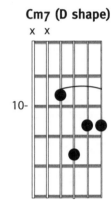

Exercise 3 shows all five CAGED shapes of the C dominant seventh chord. We've seen this chord before – its formula is 1, 3, 5, ♭7, and it's a great chord for blues and jazz.

Exercise 3

Track 6

2

C7 (C shape)	C7 (A shape)	C7 (G shape)	C7 (E shape)	C7 (D shape)

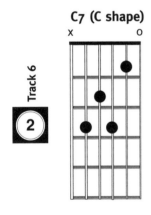 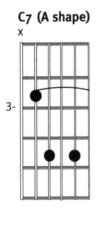  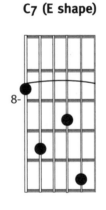 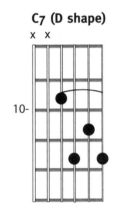

Exercise 4 includes the five CAGED shapes of the C minor seventh flat five chord (Cm7♭5). This chord is a common extension of the diminished chord and takes the formula 1, ♭3, ♭5, ♭7.

Exercise 4

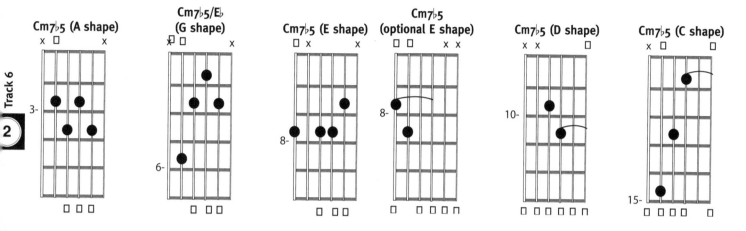

Cm7♭5 (A shape)

Cm7♭5/E♭ (G shape)

Cm7♭5 (E shape)

Cm7♭5 (optional E shape)

Cm7♭5 (D shape)

Cm7♭5 (C shape)

We can use all of the above chords as common extensions in the harmonised major scale system. Here's the order in which they appear:

Degree	Chord
I	Cmaj7
ii	Dm7
iii	Em7
IV	Fmaj7
V	Gmaj7
vi	Am7
vii	Bm7♭5

Exercise 5 illustrates all of the seventh chord extensions in the key of C major. The chords shown are in their open positions, so make sure you try other shapes in all of the other positions up and down the neck.

Electric Guitar

Exercise 5

Track 6

C maj7 (I)

Dm7 (ii)

Em7 (iii)

F maj7 (IV)

G7 (V)

Am7 (vi)

Bm7♭5 (vii)

Our final examples of the day shouldn't take you too long to look at and demonstrate the use of percussive mutes in a rhythmic pattern. Mutes can be used to great effect, and are achieved by simply laying the fretting hand across the strings. Don't press too hard, though, as you don't want to sound the notes.

Exercises 6–7 includes two rhythmic variations that use this muting technique:

Electric Guitar

Exercise 6

Exercise 7

Electric Guitar

DAY 42

WEEK 6 TEST

Well done with hanging in there this week. I really did put you through your paces, but look at what you've achieved! Before we look at this week's jam track, though, here are a few questions.

1   What's the relationship between the scales of C major and A minor?

2   What's the formula of a diminished chord?

3   How does the harmonised scale work?

4   What's the Nashville numbering system?

5   What are the seventh extensions of the harmonised scale?

WEEK 6 STUDY PIECE

Here we are again with our end-of-week jam track, a funk-style piece featuring some of the new chords you've learned this week, as well as a muted rhythm. You'll notice that I've also included the Roman numerals to indicate the progressions. Some of these are slightly different and direct you around *non-diatonic* chords – for example, the chord labelled *ii7* means you should play chord ii of G major (normally A minor) but make it a dominant seventh (ie A7). There's also a ♭vii major seventh. The seventh chord in G would be F♯ diminished, but here I've flattened it to make it a major seventh, resulting in an F major seventh chord.

The track also includes a short syncopated scale run, so take care. Aim for a cool, clean single-coil tone for maximum authenticity.

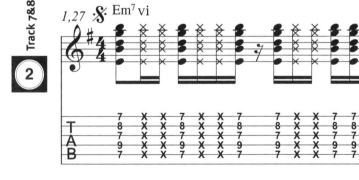

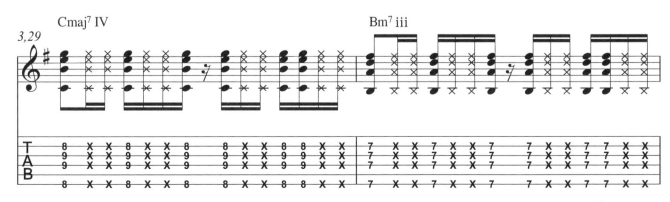

continues...

193

Electric Guitar

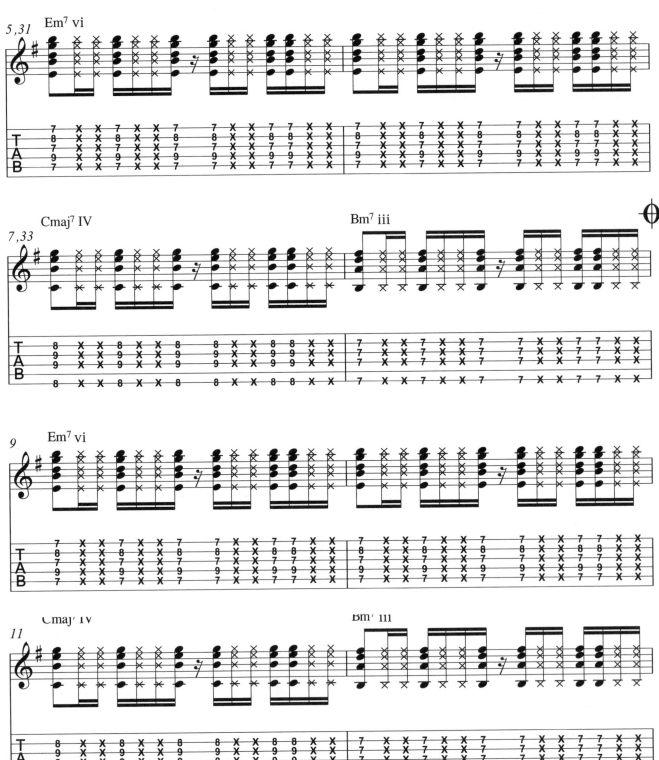

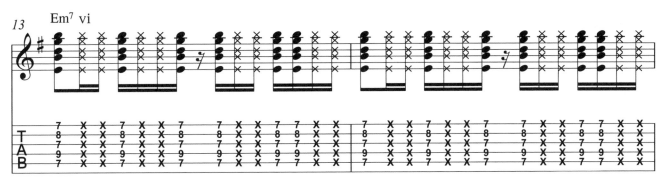

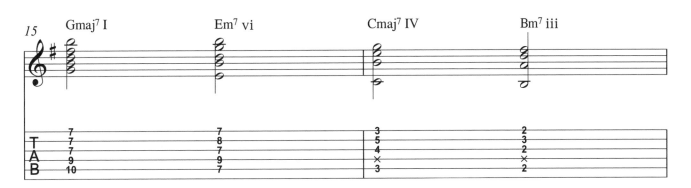

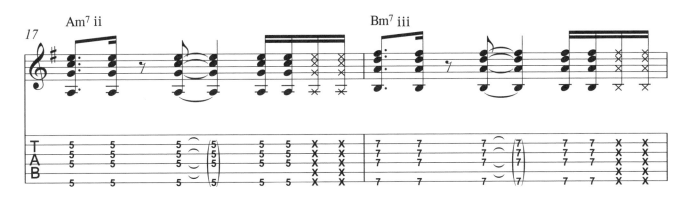

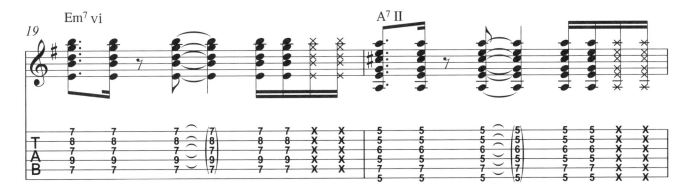

Electric Guitar

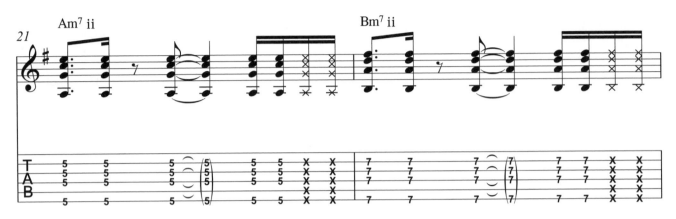

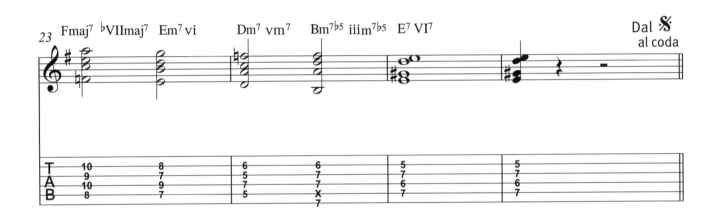

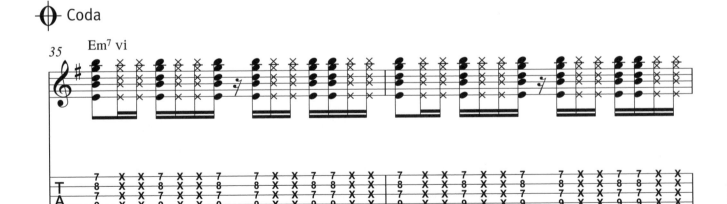

37 Bm⁷ iii

WEEK 7

OVERVIEW

We are nearly there now, and things are really starting to hot up. This week we're going to start looking at lead guitar technique and take a look at some of the scales associated with rock soloing. We'll also be looking at string bending and how to write rock riffs. In fact, here's a breakdown of what we'll be doing this week:

- Learning the minor pentatonic scale;
- Learning the blues scale;
- Learning the major pentatonic scale;
- Learning basic bending technique;
- Looking at pentatonic diads.

Electric Guitar

DAY 43: THE PENTATONIC SCALE AND EXTENDED FINGER EXERCISES

Before we get into our scale based lesson, let's look at a series of new finger exercises. So far we've looked at various chromatic sequences with a view to building up picking stamina and synchronising the left and right hands. Today we're going to push the envelope with a series of exercises that utilise every finger permutation of the fretting hand. First, let's look at the various permutations. There are 24 in total, starting off from each finger:

QUOTE FOR THE WEEK

There are a million inventive possibilities for the guitar, without adding any other appendages to it.

– Slash, Guns N' Roses

First finger start	Second finger start	Third finger start	Fourth finger start
1 2 3 4	2 1 3 4	3 1 2 4	4 2 3 1
1 2 4 3	2 1 4 3	3 1 4 2	4 2 1 3
1 3 4 2	2 4 3 1	3 2 4 1	4 1 2 3
1 3 2 4	2 4 1 3	3 2 1 4	4 1 3 2
1 4 3 2	2 3 4 1	3 4 2 1	4 3 2 1
1 4 2 3	2 3 1 4	3 4 1 2	4 3 1 2

This list of chromatic patterns should be played on every string and in every position up and down the neck. You won't be able to master an exercise of this nature in one day, and you should be using this one for many years to come.

Exercise 1 gives an example of how the first 1-2-3-4 permutation should be played.

Electric Guitar

I've shown it in only a couple of positions here, but it should be repeated until the

entire neck is covered. Make sure you use alternate picking throughout.

Exercise 1

Exercise 2 shows the 2-1-3-4 permutation. Once again, this should be performed all

over the neck, covering all positions, and again make sure you use alternate picking.

Exercise 2

Make sure you practise these exercises with a metronome so that you can gauge how much you're improving.

THE MINOR PENTATONIC SCALE

Well, here it is, the moment you've all been waiting for. Today we are going to start learning possibly the most important scale on the guitar: the minor pentatonic scale. The pentatonic scale is one of the easiest yet most effective scales to be played on guitar, which is used to great effect by the likes of Slash, Eric Clapton, Jimi Hendrix, Steve Vai, Joe Satriani and Gary Moore, to name but a few. In fact, pretty much every guitarist uses this scale, and it's incredibly effective.

As its name might suggest, the pentatonic scale is a five note scale, taking the formula 1, ♭3, 4, 5, ♭7, 1. We can apply this formula to any major scale – for example, in the key of A, we get the following notes: A, C, D, E, G and A.

The scale works great over the minor chord of the same name, as three of its five notes are chord tones, but it also works over dominant chords of the same name. Although dominant chords have a major third and the scale has a minor third, the tension between the two thirds imparts a bluesy feel.

Now that we've looked at the theory of the scale, it's time to learn to play it. The easiest way for you to get this scale under your belt is to look at it in action around the CAGED chord shapes. Exercise 3 includes pattern 1 of the A minor pentatonic scale, based on the E movable shape:

Electric Guitar

Exercise 3

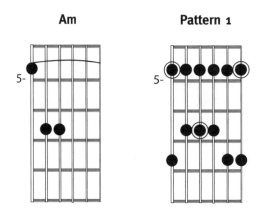

Exercise 4 shows pattern 2 of the A minor pentatonic scale, which is based on the

D minor movable shape.

Exercise 4

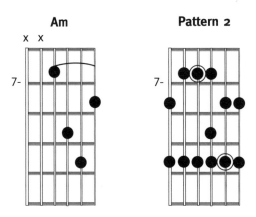

Exercise 5 includes a scale exercise that uses pattern 1. This exercise is performed

from root to root, which will enable you to move the scale into new keys.

Exercise 5

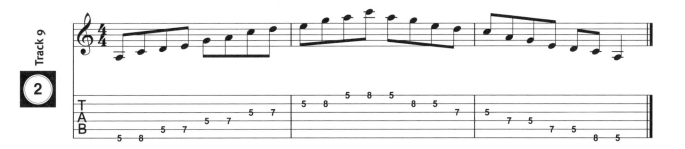

Exercise 6 is a scale exercise based on pattern 2 of the A minor pentatonic scale.

This exercise begins and ends on the lowest possible root note.

Exercise 6

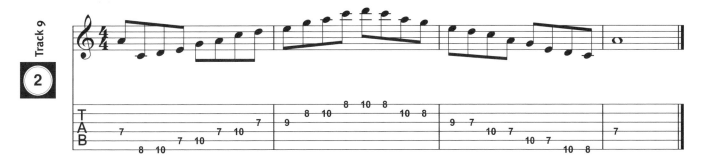

Electric Guitar

DAY 44: MORE PENTATONIC SHAPES

Today we're going to look at our final three pentatonic shapes based on the CAGED minor shapes of C, A and G minor – all in the key of A minor. Exercise 1 includes pattern 3 of the A minor pentatonic scale, based on the C minor shape of the A minor chord:

Exercise 1

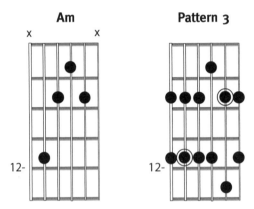

Exercise 2 includes pattern 4 of the A minor pentatonic scale, based on the A minor movable chord shape:

Exercise 2

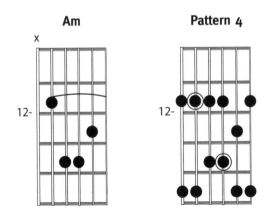

Exercise 3 is our final pentatonic shape, pattern 5, based on the G minor movable

chord shape:

Exercise 3

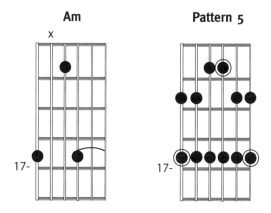

Now take a look at some more pentatonic exercises so that you can learn the

positions of the root notes for transposing purposes. Exercise 4 is based on

pattern 3 and utilises the lowest possible root note:

Exercise 4

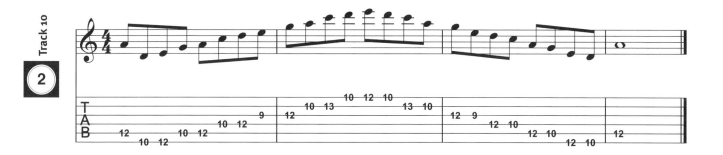

Exercise 5 uses pattern 4 of the A minor pentatonic scale, beginning and ending

with the lowest possible root note:

Electric Guitar

Exercise 5

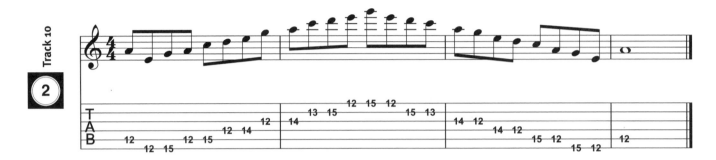

Exercise 6 includes pattern 5 of the A minor pentatonic scale, and once again is performed around the scale's lowest possible root note:

Exercise 6

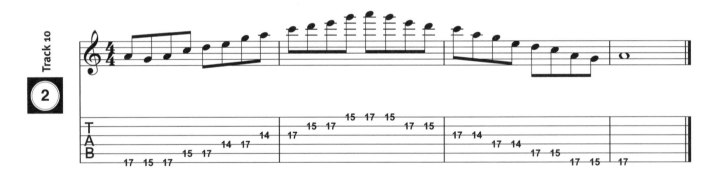

Exercise 7 includes a pentatonic picking exercise based on pattern 1. Once you have this down, make sure you practise it in all of the remaining shapes.

Exercise 7

Exercise 8 features a 12/8 pentatonic picking pattern based on pattern 1 of the A

minor pentatonic scale. Again, repeat this through all of the remaining shapes.

Exercise 8

Electric Guitar

DAY 45: UNLOCKING THE PENTATONIC FRETBOARD

One of the biggest pitfalls of learning scale patterns is becoming stuck with the scale-box shapes. The aim of learning the scales is eventually to unlock the entire fretboard and to break out of relying on boxes. One of the best ways to do this is to practise the scales on pairs of strings, moving horizontally up the neck.

Exercise 1 show all of the positions of the A minor pentatonic scale performed on the top two strings. This type of exercise will really help you to cover a lot of ground when improvising.

Exercise 1

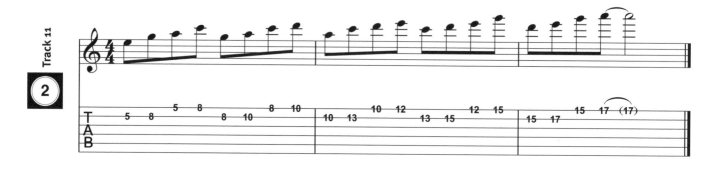

Exercise 2 includes a shifting exercise based on the second and third strings. As all of the other string pairs are tuned in *fourths*, Exercise 1 will work on these, but the second and third strings are tuned to a *major third*, so you'll have to use some different shapes:

Exercise 2

Exercise 3 demonstrates how practising on pairs of strings can help to open up the neck. This example shifts through several positions, and not only does it make for a great example but it's also a killer-sounding lick! Try using the formula shown here to shift through other shapes and positions.

Exercise 3

Another way you can practise this scale is as *diads* – ie two-note chords. This type of approach is great for breaking up single-note licks, and also for writing riffs.

Exercise 4 shows pattern 1 of the A minor pentatonic played as diads. The intervals here are a mixture of fourths and thirds.

Electric Guitar

Exercise 4

Exercise 5 is our final example of the day and illustrates how you can use the approach we looked at today to write rock riffs. Guitarists such as Ritchie Blackmore and Mark Knopfler have used this type of approach; listen to the riffs on 'Smoke On The Water', 'Burn' and 'Money For Nothing', all of which use this approach.

Exercise 5

Electric Guitar

DAY 46: THE BLUES SCALE

Now that you've started to master the minor pentatonic, you'll have probably noticed quite a few gaps in the finger patterns. The most obvious note to add to the minor pentatonic is the flattened fifth, also known as the *blues note*. The addition of this note can really change the sound of the pentatonic scale, and you can certainly hear where it gets its name! To get some idea of how this new *blues scale* works, listen to the classic Cream track 'Sunshine Of Your Love'.

Exercises 1–5 include all of the positions of the A blues scale based on the five CAGED shapes of the A dominant seventh chord. This scale should be pretty straightforward for you to learn, as all you need to do is add one note to the scale shapes you already know.

Track 12

②

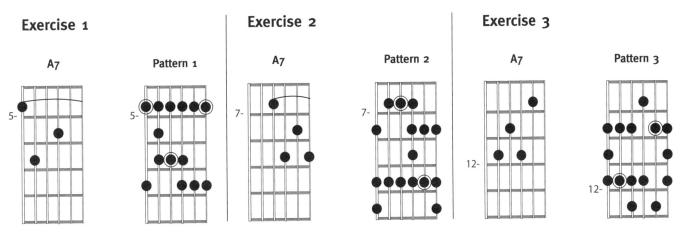

Electric Guitar

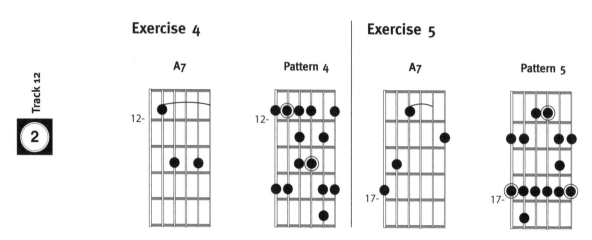

Exercise 6 is an example of how we can shift through several positions of the A blues scale. Try to come up with similar licks that use all of the other positions of the blues scale.

Exercise 6

Exercise 7 is yet another useful blues scale lick for you to try, this one using patterns further up the neck. Shifting to higher register patterns can really help to build excitement in a solo.

Exercise 7

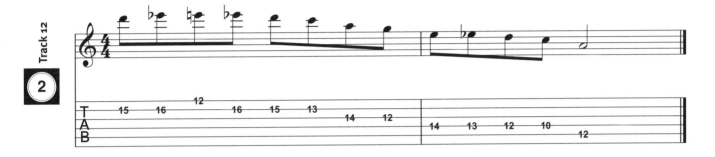

Electric Guitar

DAY 47: THE MAJOR PENTATONIC SCALE

Today we are going to look at another pentatonic scale, the major pentatonic. This scale has a very different sound from the minor pentatonic and follows the scale formula 1, 2, 3, 5, 6, 1.

One of advantages of this scale is that, like the relative major/minor scales, we actually use the same shapes that we learned for the minor pentatonic but treat another note as the root note. This type of scale is often used in rock and country, although it's actually disregarded by many guitarists early on in their careers. Listen to the opening solo of the Guns N' Roses version of 'Knocking On Heaven's Door', where Slash uses the scale to great effect, blending smooth lines with searing string bends.

Exercises 1–5 include all of the five patterns of the A major pentatonic scale based on the five CAGED major scale shapes. When practising these shapes, try to relate them to the minor pentatonic scale.

Track 13

2

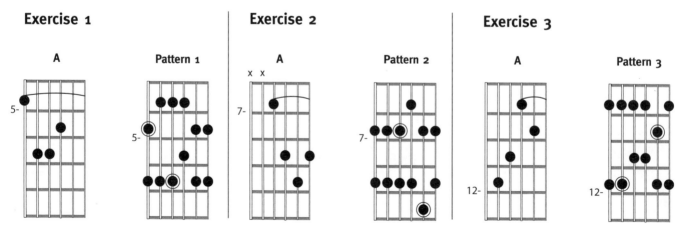

214

Electric Guitar

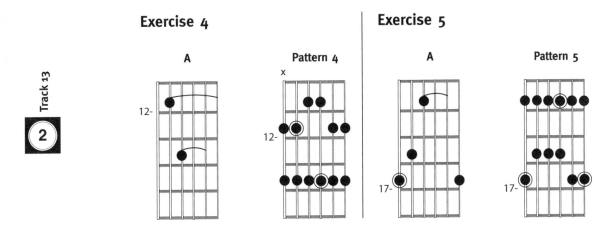

Exercise 4

A

Pattern 4

Exercise 5

A

Pattern 5

Exercises 6–7 provide a couple of helpful major pentatonic licks to help you on your way. When you've got the hang of them, experiment with melodic figures of your own in various positions.

Exercise 6

Exercise 7

Electric Guitar

 I should really mention that, when you've finally learned both major and minor pentatonics and the blues scale, you should practise all of the shapes in every key using the cycle of fourths. Try practising them as individual keys, five shapes at a time, and then one shape per key, keeping the scales in close proximity. This will help you when playing over chord changes, and will also help you to gain knowledge of the fretboard.

DAY 48: MORE STRING-PAIR PRACTICE AND STRING BENDS

I mentioned in yesterday's lesson the importance of practising our pentatonic major/minor and blues scales in every key all over the fretboard. We've already looked at practising the minor pentatonic on all pairs of strings, so now it's time to look at the major pentatonic and blues scales in the same way. The exercises that follow shouldn't present too many problems, as the shapes are similar to, if not the same as, the minor pentatonic scale.

Exercise 1 is based on the A major pentatonic scale played on the top two strings, shifting through all of the five CAGED patterns. Once you have this one down, remember to practise it on the remaining string pairs, but remember that the G and B strings are tuned to a major third, not a fourth, so be sure to alter the shapes.

Exercise 1

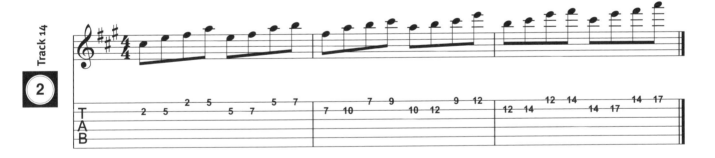

Exercise 2 includes the blues scale performed in all of the five CAGED scale positions. This example is a little more difficult than the major and minor pentatonic scales due to the fact that there are some three-note-per-string patterns involved. Once you've practised this one, be sure to try it with the other string groups.

Electric Guitar

Exercise 2

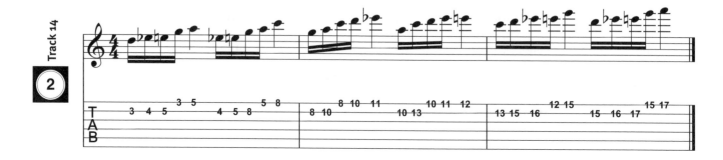

Now we're going to look at a new lead guitar tool, and a very expressive one at that: *string bending*. The idea here is to fret a note and raise the pitch to another by either pushing it up or pulling it down (depending on the string). This is a very expressive technique, and players such as Dave Gilmour and Jeff Beck use it to great effect.

There are several possible approaches to string bending. Probably the most accurate is to fret a note and then move the fretting-hand wrist and fingers to raise its pitch. (I would also suggest placing other fingers behind the finger fretting the note to give it extra strength, as some strings are pretty tough to bend.)

Electric Guitar

When bending a note, you don't just bend at random; you need to bend up to other notes within a scale, preferably those that appear in the same progression. When reading a bend on tab, the first note is written and then the target note will be shown in brackets, as shown below.

Exercise 3 illustrates some standard string bends around the A minor pentatonic scale. Take care with the pitches of the bends, making sure they're neither sharp nor flat.

Exercise 3

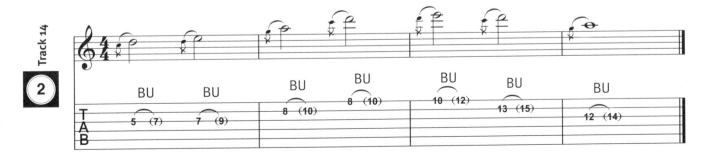

219

Electric Guitar

DAY 48 STUDY PIECE

The study piece in Exercise 4 is based on a 12-bar blues, and the main aim here is to practise string bending, working it into some form of melodic context. I've tried to outline the chord changes with string bends, targeting specific notes in each chord. Once you've got this piece under your fingers, experiment with some ideas of your own.

Exercise 4

DAY 49

WEEK 7 TEST

Here we are again with another end-of-week test and study piece. This week included quite a few new scales and techniques, so let's just take a few moments to see how much has sunk in.

1   How many notes are there in a pentatonic scale?

2   What's the formula for the major pentatonic scale?

3   What's the formula for the minor pentatonic scale?

4   What note is added to the minor pentatonic scale to produce the blues scale?

5   What's the interval between the G and B strings called?

Electric Guitar

WEEK 7 STUDY PIECE

You're in for a real treat with Week 7's end-of-week jam track. For this one I looked at bands like AC/DC and The Darkness for inspiration, mixing up rocking power chords with pentatonic riffs. The outro (ie the end section) of the track includes a short string-bending solo, so make sure you invite other members of the household in to witness your progress – in just seven weeks! When you've polished the track, try out some of your own licks and bending ideas.

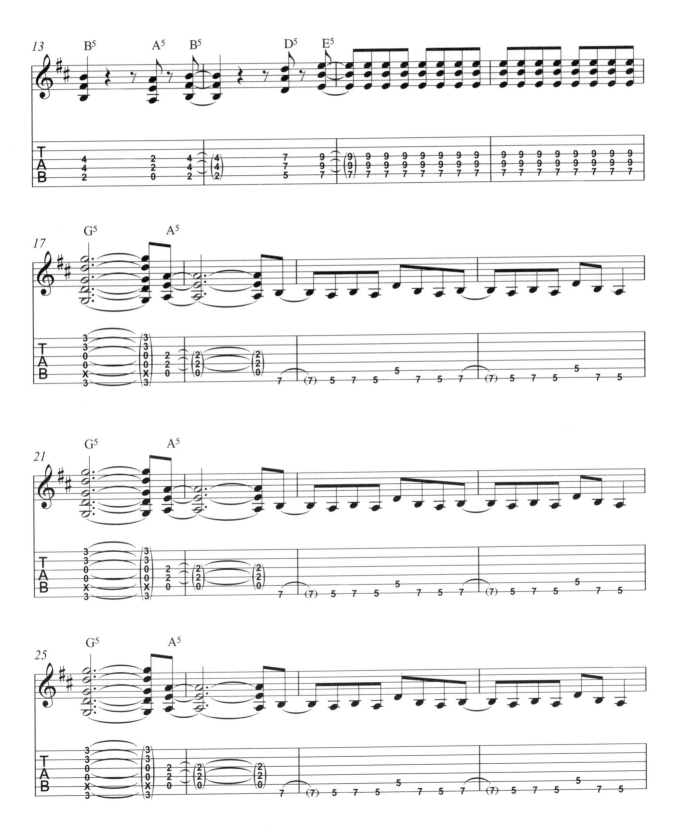

Electric Guitar

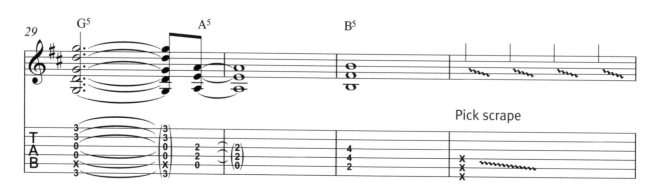

WEEK 8

OVERVIEW

OK, here we are with our final week of lessons. After this, you're on your own! This week's lessons tie up a few loose ends and introduce a couple of new approaches to learning and playing scales. Anyway, without further ado, here is a breakdown of what to expect in your final week:

- Hammer-on and pull-off ideas;
- Major and minor arpeggios;
- Two-handed tapping;
- Three-note-per-string scales.

Electric Guitar

DAY 50: LEFT-HAND SLURS

To get this week under way, I've decided to revisit the blues, but to give it a much more sophisticated sound by using some slightly more advanced chords. The chords we're going to look at here comprise a mixture of sixth and ninth chords. The cool thing about these chords is that you need to learn only two shapes in total. Using these types of chords will give your blues playing a slightly jazzy edge, reminiscent of Robben Ford's playing.

Exercise 1 includes the chords of A9 and A6. You should notice straight away that both chords use the same shape; the ninth simply shifts up two frets to become the sixth.

Exercise 1

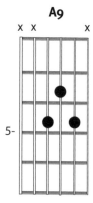

Exercise 2 includes the chords of D6 and D9. These chords also share the same shape as each other and are played simply by barring the top three strings.

Exercise 2

Track 17

2

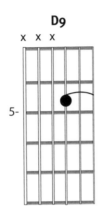

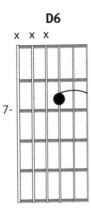

Exercise 3 is our final set of chords, E6 and E9. Once again, these chords share shapes, and as a matter of fact the E9 chord is exactly the same as the D6.

Exercise 3

Track 17

2

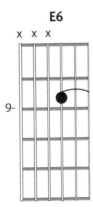

Now let's look at some more string-bending ideas. So far we've looked at only the whole-tone bend. Exercise 4 is a lick that includes a quarter-tone bend:

Electric Guitar

If you cast your mind back, you'll remember I mentioned that the A minor pentatonic actually works over the A dominant seventh chord, the clash between the major third of the chord and the minor third of the scale producing a blues feel. Well, we can imply a tension-and-release sound by playing a minor third over the major third of a chord in a soloing context. As shown in Exercise 4, play the minor third and then bend it slightly to imply the major third, releasing the tension of the clashing notes. Here the note of C♮ is bent very slightly sharp to imply C♯, giving the lick a very bluesy tone.

Exercise 4

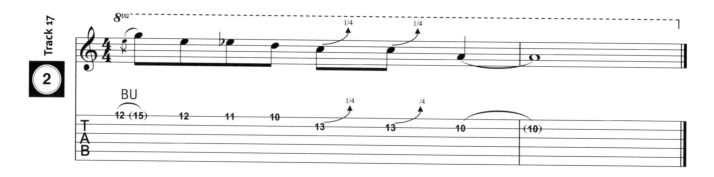

Exercise 5 includes some unison bends. Here we fret two notes but bend up the pitch of the note on the lower string of the pair. This type of bending is used a lot by country guitarists, but has also been borrowed by us rock guys!

Exercise 5

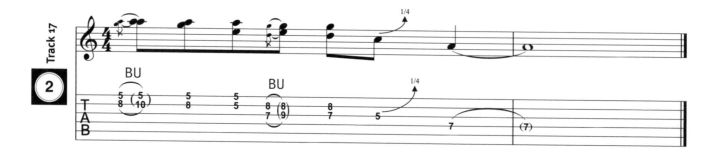

Electric Guitar

Now we're going to take a look at some left-hand techniques. So far I've concentrated a lot on the picking hand, but there are a few things you can do with the fretting hand, namely *hammer-ons* and *pull-offs*. The idea of the hammer-on is that you play a note and then 'hammer' down the next finger on the fretting hand to sound the next note, producing a smooth transition between notes.

The pull-off, meanwhile, is essentially the reverse of the hammer-on. Simply pull a finger away to sound a note fretted behind it. A combination of hammer-ons and pull-offs is called *legato*, and can be heard in the playing style of rock guitarist Joe Satriani.

Care has to be taken when playing hammer-ons and pull-offs, as it's very easy to sound unwanted strings, so it's important that you develop a good muting technique to ensure that your lines are smooth and clean. Another term for these combined techniques is *left-hand slurs*.

Exercise 6 is a basic hammer-on exercise based on the A minor pentatonic scale. Make sure you experiment with your muting technique so that unwanted strings don't sound.

Exercise 6

Electric Guitar

Exercise 7 is an extension of the previous hammer-on exercise and is great for

building stamina:

Exercise 7

DAY 51: PULL-OFF LICKS AND ADVANCED BLUES

Today we're going to look at some licks that use the pull-off technique we looked at

yesterday. We're also going to add sixth and ninth chords to a blues progression.

Exercise 1 is a pull-off sequence based on the A minor pentatonic scale. It might

take a bit of practice to get this exercise smooth and rhythmically consistent.

Exercise 1

Exercise 2 is yet another (slightly longer) pull-off exercise. This one is designed to

help build stamina:

Exercise 2

Electric Guitar

Exercises 3–4 are combination licks that use both hammer-ons and pull-offs. These types of licks are great to have in your repertoire, so make sure you remember them.

Exercise 3

Exercise 4

DAY 51 STUDY PIECE

Today's study piece is a 12-bar blues. However, instead of using basic chords or riffs, this one makes use of our new jazzy-sounding sixth and ninth chords. Also, pay close attention here to another new technique, the *slide*, where you strike the chord and then slide it into the correct position. The first chord of each cycle here is performed with a slide.

Exercise 5

Electric Guitar

DAY 52: BASIC ARPEGGIOS

You've already come across the term *arpeggio* – used to describe the playing of a chord as individual notes – and we can include arpeggios in our soloing, as shown in today's lesson. Arpeggios are a very melodic way of outlining chords and progressions, and guitarists such as Steve Morse, Yngwie Malmsteen and Ritchie Blackmore have all made great use of them in their playing.

Arpeggios can also be used to imply more sophisticated harmonies, but this is something to develop much later on. For now, we're going to look at a selection of arpeggio patterns, plus a melodic study. The arpeggios shown in the next few exercises use the same formulas as the chords they imply: the major (1, 3, 5) and the minor (1, ♭3, 5).

Exercises 1–2 include two different major arpeggio patterns that outline the arpeggios of A and D major, respectively:

Exercise 1

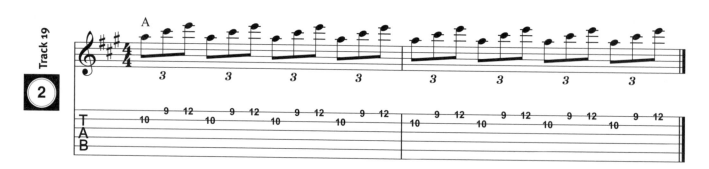

234

Electric Guitar

Exercise 2

Exercises 3–4 show two different shapes of A minor and D minor arpeggios,

respectively:

Exercise 3

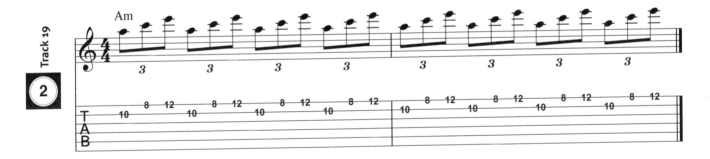

Exercise 4

Electric Guitar

To round off today's lesson I've included a short Steve Morse-style arpeggio progression that will help you to practise your arpeggios in a melodic environment. This entire exercise is to be performed using alternate picking. I've also included an extra E7/G♯ arpeggio to give a slightly neo-classical flavour.

Exercise 5

236

DAY 53: COMBINATION LICKS AND TAPPING

Today's lesson features some combination licks to give you a taste of how all of the techniques we've looked at so far will sound when applied together. We'll also look at how to include both major and minor scales in your pentatonic riffs, as well as adding some real fire to your playing with a few basic tapping licks.

As we've seen, both major and minor pentatonic scales are arrived at by using notes from the major and minor scales. These scales can also be mixed up to great effect.

The only notes missing from the minor pentatonic scale to turn it into a natural minor are the second and the sixth. The two scales work hand in hand, and you can really spice up your pentatonic scales by adding these extra notes.

Exercise 1 is a lick that combines both the minor scale and the minor pentatonic scale. I've also included some bends, hammer-ons and pull-offs.

Exercise 1

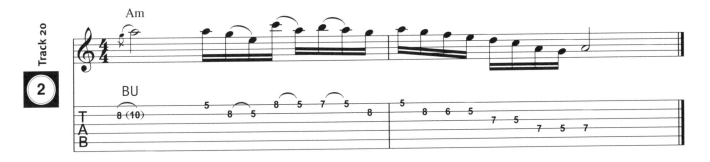

The only notes missing from the major pentatonic to turn it into the major scale are the fourth and seventh. Exercise 2 is a major/major pentatonic scale combination lick.

Electric Guitar

Exercise 2

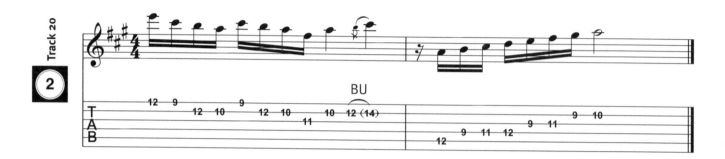

Two-handed tapping is a technique that was popularised by Eddie Van Halen. The idea is that you tap an extra note with a finger of the picking hand, executed in a similar way to a hammer-on and pull-off. First, hammer the finger down on the desired fret position, then pull off the tapping finger to sound a note held by the left hand. I would suggest tapping with the second finger, and using the first finger to hold the pick. Make sure you pay attention to muting the open strings!

This technique is actually a lot easier than it might seem, and once you've got it under your belt, you can use it to play some very exciting and fast licks. Check out the awesome track 'Eruption' from the *Van Halen I* album.

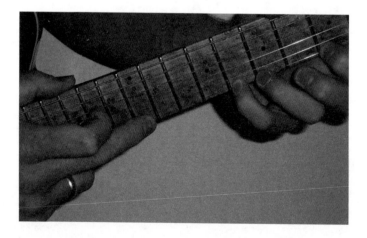

Electric Guitar

Exercise 3 demonstrates the tapping technique. Here it's used to perform an A

minor arpeggio in a triplet rhythm:

Exercise 3

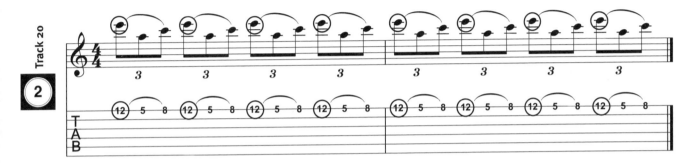

Exercise 4 is another tapping lick that's based on the Van Halen approach, used

here to play a series of arpeggios. Notice how some arpeggios are sounded by

simply shifting the tapping finger up one fret:

Exercise 4

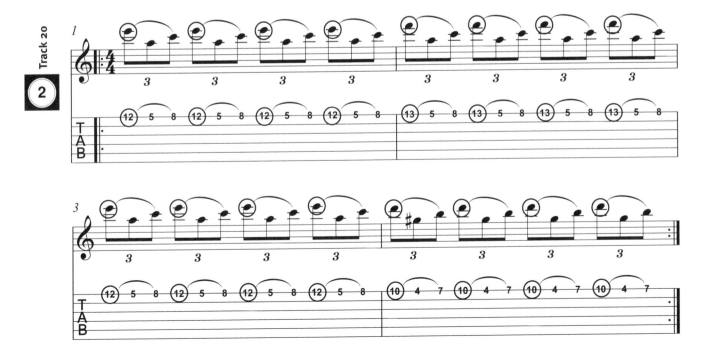

Electric Guitar

Here's our final tapping exercise – yet another variation on our original pattern. In this exercise, the order of the notes played by the fretting hand is changed every other beat. This is a very effective-sounding pattern and works great at speed:

Exercise 5

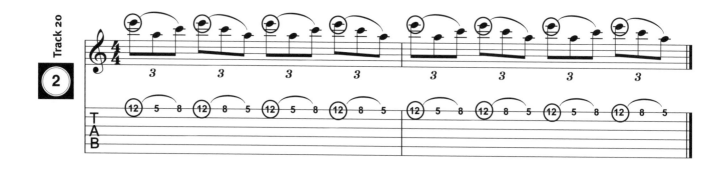

DAY 54: THREE-NOTE-PER-STRING SCALES

Many guitarists favour a technique known as *three-note-per-string scales*, whereby the major scale is arranged into a series of three-note sequences, making fast picking and legato runs easier to play. In fact, the CAGED major scale shapes you learned earlier can be arranged in a manner that will produce these patterns, which should be linked together to cover the entire fretboard. You can then start from each note of the scale on the sixth string and play a series of seven three-note-per-string patterns.

When the scales are arranged like this, we end up with not only the whole major scale but all fingerings for all seven of the major *modes*, too. Talking of which, I don't want to blind you with science too much, but here's a brief description of modes.

The idea behind modes is that we can negotiate a diatonic chord progression while playing in one key for all of the positions on the fretboard. In theory, we simply stick to the same scale and the accompanying progression decides the mode that's being played. If you play over chord ii, mode ii will be heard. If you play over chord IV, then mode IV will be heard, and so on. The modes can also be sounded by the intervals that make up each of the seven shapes. Here's a list of the seven modes:

Degree	Mode (Tonality)
I	C Ionian (major)
ii	D Dorian (minor)
iii	E Phrygian (minor)

Electric Guitar

Degree	Mode (Tonality)
IV	F Lydian (major)
V	G Mixolydian (major)
vi	A Aeolian (minor)
vii	B Locrian (diminished)

Exercises 1–7 show all of the seven modal three-note-per-string shapes. These shapes can be played over any of the chords in the C major harmonised scale and combined to cover the entire fretboard in one key. Learn them well – they're very important.

Exercise 1

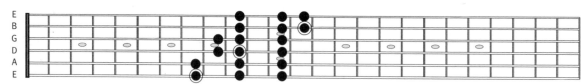

C major pattern 1 (C Ionian)

Exercise 2

C major pattern 2 (D Dorian)

Exercise 3

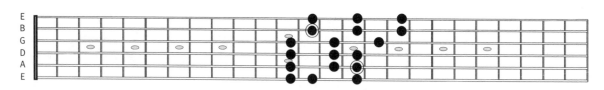

C major pattern 3 (E Phrygian)

Electric Guitar

Exercise 4

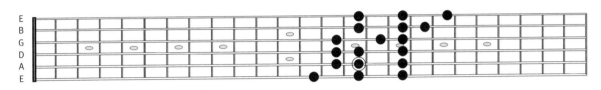

C major pattern 4 (F Lydian)

Exercise 5

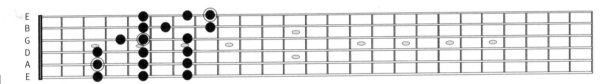

C major pattern 5 (G Mixolydian)

Exercise 6

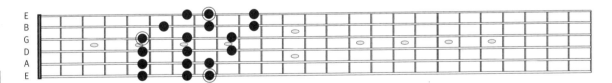

C major pattern 6 (A Aeolian)

Exercise 7

C major pattern 7 (B Locrian)

Electric Guitar

DAY 55: THREE-NOTE-PER-STRING RUNS

Today we're going to look at combining our three note per string scales with various techniques to form runs, using both alternate picking and hammer-ons and pull-offs to move around the fretboard. We'll also look at shifting position so that you don't get stuck in the chord boxes!

Exercise 1 is a run that uses a repeating triplet shape based on the A Aeolian mode. Make sure you use strict alternate picking.

Exercise 1

Exercise 2 is a single-string pattern that shifts through all of the positions of the C major scale on the top two strings. Again, alternate picking should be used.

Exercise 2

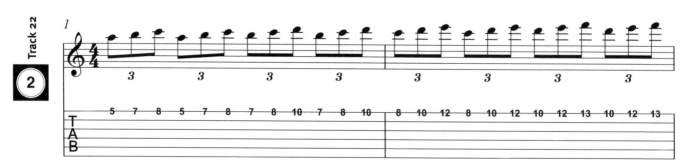

continues...

Exercise 2 continued

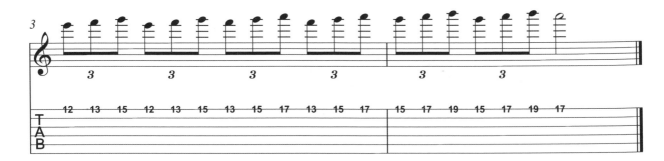

Exercise 3 is a descending picking figure to be played on the top two strings, through all positions of the C major scale. Make sure you use one finger per fret, as you did with the chromatic patterns. Try this exercise over the A minor chord – it sounds killer!

Exercise 3

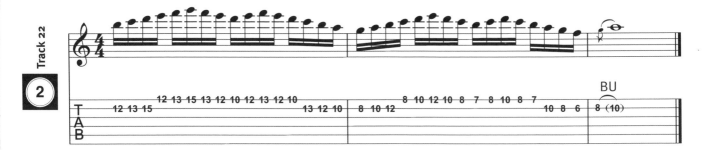

Exercise 4 includes a fast ascending run that uses the C major scale, performed with a group of three-note hammer-ons:

Exercise 4

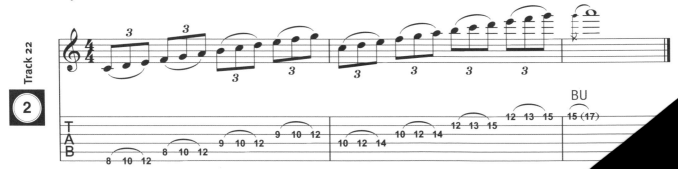

Electric Guitar

DAY 56

WEEK 8 TEST

Congratulations! You made it. Here you are at the final test of your Crash Course in electric guitar. We've covered a lot of material this week, so let's see how you did.

1 What is a unison bend?

2 What's the difference between a hammer-on and a pull-off?

3 What is tapping?

4 What are the names of the seven modes?

he minor pentatonic and minor scales differ?

Electric Guitar

DAY 56 STUDY PIECE

Today' piece is really whatever you want to make it. As you can hear on the CD track, I recorded an A/B riff and basically jammed over the two sections using all of the lead techniques found in the book. This will hopefully give you some ideas – but, of course, the rest is up to you.

You should be able to use this blank track as an empty canvas for a very long time, using it to practise licks and improve your improvisational skills. To give you a helping hand, for the first section try using A minor pentatonic/A minor, and for the second section try E minor pentatonic/E minor. Have a go at developing melodies and gradually work on your technique. Good luck!

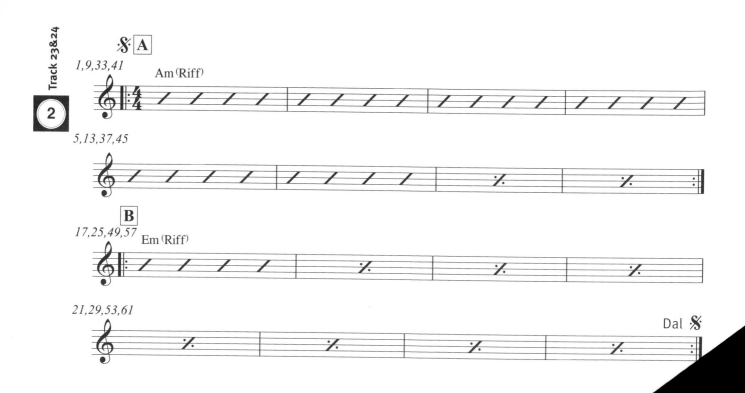

GOODBYE AND GOOD LUCK!

Well, that's it from me. I hope you've enjoyed this book. There was a lot to get

through, and some of this info will probably be part of your practice for many years

to come. Try not to think of this book as just a Crash Course, but also as a scale and

chord reference manual that you'll continue to use as a study guide.

All that's left for me to do now is say goodbye for now, and good luck. You've just

touched the tip of the iceberg. Now it's up to you to follow your own musical path,

and to enjoy playing the kind of music you want to play.

3/12 (182414)